One Pilot's

Flying the CBI Hump – Ag Aviation
Airline Pilot Training School

By
Thomas E. Herrod

Copyright © 2013 Thomas E. Herrod
All Rights Reserved.

No part of this book may be reproduced, stored in a retrieval system, or transmitted by any means without written permission of the author.

ISBN-13: 978-1492113546
ISBN-10: 1492113549

LCCN: 2013915417
CreateSpace Independent Publishing Platform, North Charleston, SC

ABOUT THE AUTHOR

The author was born in 1921 and took his first flying lesson in the summer of 1936. He joined the Army Air Corps in 1942 and logged over 3000 hours during WW II. He was awarded two Air Medals, the Distinguished Flying Cross and the Presidential Unit Citation. He left the U.S. Air Force Reserve in 1953 with the rank of Major. The author spent 13 years in Agriculture Aviation, Followed by 10 years operating his Airline Pilot Training School in Billings, Montana. His FAA ratings are: Airline Transport Pilot, Airplane Single & Multiengine Land, Commercial Privileges: Airplane Single Engine Sea and Glider, Ground Instructor: Advanced Instrument, Mechanic: Airframe and Powerplant, and Flight Instructor: Airplane Single & Multiengine, Instrument Airplane and Glider. He also served several years as an FAA flight examiner.

PREFACE

This is a true story of **"One Pilot's Life"**, from 1935 to the 1970's. This was a time in aviation history, when aviation advanced from the most dangerous profession, to one of the safest. It was also a time when needle, ball and airspeed indicators were the only dependable, useable instruments when flying in bad weather. Today, glass cockpits make instrument flying like flying in clear weather. It was also a time when you had to fly at ten thousand feet or below in all weather conditions; today, we fly above thirty thousand feet and above the bad weather. It was a time when the low frequency range was the primary navigation system; today, all navigational information is displayed on a glass cockpit, showing your position utilizing the Global Positioning System (GPS). It was a time when it took an experienced pilot to understand low frequency voice transmissions; today, voice transmissions are very clear thanks to VHF's. Early aviation was a time when your filed flight plan was just a small strip of paper on the controller's desk; today, the controller can follow you on his monitor with all the information displayed. It was a time, when during taking off, there was a short, dangerous period between takeoff speed and engine-out controllable speed. Today, airlines must have enough runway length for takeoff to be able to stop or continue a safe takeoff with an engine out. These are some of the reasons why the airline pilot profession is now one of the safest professions.

ACKNOWLEDGEMENTS

Mere words cannot fully express my gratitude to my wife Judy, for her love, help, support and encouragement during the writing of this book, and her many hours of preparing this book for publication. She was a flight instructor in my Airline Pilot Training School and since then we have enjoyed many years together. She helped temper bitter memories and the lingering hatred toward a former enemy.

My friend, Carolyn Pierce, a retired English teacher, edited this book and corrected all of my grammatical and spelling errors. She encouraged the addition of more detail in a way that made my story more interesting. She caused technical aviation jargon to be changed so the non-aviation reader would enjoy reading the story.

Thanks to Dean Davis for his help in writing this book. He is a pilot, with a degree in electrical engineering, who has devoted his life to aviation. Not only has he done research work with test pilots that became astronauts, he has worked at Honeywell on the Guidance, Control and Sequencing Computer for the NASA Mars Viking program. His name will always be on a gold plate, on the Viking, resting on Mars.

The China-Burma-India Hump Pilots Association was active for over 56 years. It is the members of this organization that collected pictures and had them published in four volumes, by Turner Publishing Company in Paducah, KY. Some of these pictures and the detailed explanation of what you see make this story more interesting.

Table of Contents

About the Author	iii
Preface	v
Acknowledgements	vi

Part I - My Early Years in Aviation — 1

Chapter 1: Introduction to Aviation 1932-1939	3
Chapter 2: Civil Pilot Training 1939-1941	9
Chapter 3: Army Air Corps Cadet 1941-1942	17
Chapter 4: Victorville Army Air Base 1942	31
Chapter 5: Columbia Army Air Base 1942	39
Chapter 6: Return to Columbia 1943	51

Part II - CBI Hump Pilot — 55

Chapter 7: Orders	57
Chapter 8: Gaya, India	63
Chapter 9: Chabua, India Air Base	65
Chapter 10: The Black Market	71
Chapter 11: Passenger Flights	75
Chapter 12: Weather Pilots	81
Chapter 13: An Instrument Takeoff	85
Chapter 14: 20,000 Feet Looking Up at Mountains	87
Chapter 15: 38 Enemy Aircraft Overhead	89
Chapter 16: Barry Goldwater Logs Combat Time	91
Chapter 17: Heavy Icing	97
Chapter 18: Pilot Combat Fatigue	101
Chapter 19: Battle for Imphal Valley	109
Chapter 20: 803rd Medical Air Evac Transport Squadron	115
Chapter 21: The Final Hump Trips	127
Chapter 22: Orders Home	131

Part III – Crop Spraying, Aerial Contract Spraying, and Airline Pilot Training School — 133

Chapter 23: ATC Ferry Command 1944	135
Chapter 24: Eastern Airlines 1945	141
Chapter 25: Crop Dusting 1948	151
Chapter 26: Aerial Agriculture Business 1950-1953	157
Chapter 27: New Piper PA-20 1953	163
Chapter 28: Aerial Agriculture Corporation 1957	167
Chapter 29: Government Contract Spraying 1957-1961	171
Chapter 30: Chemical Business 1958-1960	177
Chapter 31: The Last Contracts 1961	181
Chapter 32: Airline Pilot School 1961-1969	185
Chapter 33: Looking Back	195

Part I

My Early Years in Aviation

CHAPTER 1
Introduction to Aviation 1932-1939

Would anyone believe that a movie could shape the entire life of an eleven-year-old kid? It was in 1932, at the height of the Great Depression, when Howard Hughes completed his film, "Hells Angels", starring Jean Harlow. It was one of the first talkie movies ever made, and it was all about aviation combat flying during World War I. I was that eleven-year old kid who saw that movie seven times. All the aerial scenes were very real, and they had to use up a lot of World War I aircraft in making this movie.

It was not long after this movie came out that a couple of boys next door built a glider. It was nothing more than a wing and tail assembly mounted on a wood frame with an open seat, stick and rudder controls in front. During the summer, on weekends, everyone in the neighborhood would gather on a nearby open hillside to help launch the glider. The power for the launch was provided by two long bungee cords pulled tight by a few dozen men. Someone would hold the wings level, and when they got the two bungee cords as tight as possible, the man behind the tail would release the glider, and off it would fly down the hill. While too young to help in any way, I felt it was exciting, and the seed was firmly planted for me to become a pilot and fly airplanes.

For the next few years, my spare time was used building kites and model airplanes. All the kids could build and fly kites, but only two of us were building and flying model airplanes. We would build the model airplanes using balsa wood and tissue paper, powering them with rubber bands. The most successful one was a twin pusher model that flew about two city blocks (without a tailwind).

If someone could build a big enough kite, why couldn't he use it as a glider? It seemed logical to me, so inside our two-car garage, I built a big kite. It was so big, in fact, that it would not go through either of the two garage doors until it was disassembled and reassembled outside the garage. With the help of some neighborhood kids, we carried the kite a few blocks to a cliff that was about twenty feet high. Then, holding onto the kite and running fast, over the cliff I went. It was the most unsuccessful flight ever made throughout my flying career, but the kite and I came through unharmed.

Later that same day, we all wanted to see the big kite fly, so we carried the kite back to an open field behind our house. By the time we got there, tied my father's trotline to the kite and assembled a long tail, it was dark, and a strong wind had come up. We thought the kite should have a red light, so we tied my father's kerosene red railroad lantern to the end of the long tail. By this time, it was very dark, and the wind was blowing very hard. With the kerosene lantern burning brightly, it took several boys to hold the kite in launch position, and several more to hold the line. The kite was launched. It went straight up very fast and very high, with the red lantern burning brightly. It then came straight down very fast, crashing into the ground, completely destroying the kite and Dad's railroad lantern. This made two aeronautical failures in one day.

During this time I was a junior high school student. The school was only three blocks from downtown, and after school it would be time to go to the best corner in town and sell the evening newspaper. I would stand on the corner, holding a newspaper high overhead, yelling, "READ ALL ABOUT IT - JAPANESE ATTACK CHINA" or what-ever news that would sell the newspapers. In order to sell newspapers, the newsboy had to read and understand the news and what was going on in the world. Reading about Italy's invasion of Ethiopia, Japan's invasion of China, and the rise of Hitler to power in Germany, provided an insight into the future that other kids and most adults did not have. This insight would prove to be important in planning and shaping my future.

Often aviation was involved, and those stories would be read in great detail. My heroes were pilots such as Charles Lindberg, Eddie Rickenbacker, Wiley Post and Amelia Earhart. These stories only reinforced my desire to learn to fly and become a pilot.

The summer of 1935 was the time for me to do something about learning to fly. Using my bicycle as transportation, I was off to Adams Field, (Little Rock, Arkansas's, airport), to find a job working for flying time. There was no way I could pay cash. Adams Field was an eight-mile bicycle ride from home. As I came into the entrance to the airport, I could see a large hangar on the right with a fence separating the parking lot from the airport. The runway was a large grass field. Straight ahead of the entrance was a small white wood frame terminal with a small restaurant.

It took a few days to get acquainted and meet some pilots. They were very interesting. Some were World War I pilots; some were crop duster pilots; and most were barnstormers. The first pilot who took an interest in me was Earl Thomas. He had a straight wing Stinson that he used for barnstorming; his Stinson had seven seats, but was only legal for five. The busy days at the airport were Saturdays and Sundays, when crowds would gather to watch the airplanes fly. The barnstormers would sell airplane rides for one-dollar.

For the most part, aviation aircraft and pilots had been unregulated, but around 1934 Congress established the Civil Aeronautics Administration. For the first time in aviation history, the government was trying to establish control over the aircraft and pilots. They assigned CAA inspectors to administer new regulations, give pilots flight check rides, and issue pilot licenses. As always, the aviation people resisted, but as always, the government was winning. Earl Thomas identified the inspector and the inspector's car. Then he gave me a job of standing watch at the airport entrance on Saturday and Sunday. If "Little John", as the inspector was called, came through the entrance, I was to signal the pilots on the flight line so they could quickly remove the extra two seats from the straight wing Stinson, thereby making it legal.

Late one Sunday evening, the sun was starting to set, and things had slowed down. Earl said, "Tom, come on. We are going to take that Porterfield Zephyr to the hangar the short way." The Porterfield Zephyr looked much like what would later become the famous Piper Cub, but unlike the Piper Cub, the wheels had no brakes or tail wheel. It had a tailskid that served as a brake: when power was applied with an up elevator, it caused the tailskid to dig into the ground. To release the so-called brake, the pilot applied power and down elevator to lift the tailskid off the ground.

Since we were only three-hundred feet from the hangar apron, I knew that it would be my first flight in an airplane. Earl got into the front seat, and I got into the back seat of this tandem two-place airplane. Someone propped us to start the engine, and with the airplane headed toward the open field, Earl said, "Take off." I opened the throttle, and the airplane moved forward but ended up making a ninety-degree left turn. Earl cut the power, turned the airplane back toward the open field, and said, "OK, try it again." This time, with the help of some right rudder, I made my first takeoff.

The next thirty minutes were spent doing turns and flying around the city. Finally, Earl said, "I've got it." He took the controls and flew close to the ground, flying straight toward a big, long, high cottonseed storage building located on the edge of the airport. He flew up one side of that building and down the other side, and then landed on the hangar apron. That's what he called "taking the plane to the hangar the short way".

It was one excided kid who jumped on his bicycle and rode home to tell his parents all about flying the airplane. The very next day my parents bought a paid-up Metropolitan life insurance policy on me, with themselves as beneficiaries. They figured that it would be only a matter of time before they would need it, because flying an airplane in the thirties was about the most dangerous thing anybody could do. It's now been sixty-eight years, and the life insurance policy is still there, unused. Someday, someone will collect the two-hundred-and-fifty-dollar value of the Metropolitan life insurance policy.

There was a pilot flying at Adams Field, whose name was Watt King. He had a good-looking airplane, so I offered to work for a flight lesson. He took me to the hangar and said, "Clean up those crop dusters, and I'll give you a flight lesson." There were about twenty planes in the hangar that had been dusting with calcium arsenic, and they were very dirty. In those days the crop duster pilots chewed tobacco to keep the arsenic out of their system, and they would spit on the cockpit floor. The worst part of cleaning those planes was scraping all the tobacco off the cockpit floor.

After completing the aircraft cleaning, I went to find Watt King, only to learn that he had left about four days earlier. He didn't even own any of the dusters, and he was not coming back. This was beginning to be a hard way to learn to fly, but I did learn a lot about crop duster aircraft. A few years later Watt King was killed in a plane crash after joining the RAF.

The two pilots who became my best friends were Earl Thomas and Ed Shepard. When the pilots would go to the terminal restaurant, one or the other would say, "Come on, Tom. I'm going to buy you a Coke." What a thrill it was just to sit there and listen to the pilots talk flying. I could make a five-cent Coke last three hours. One of the pilots had flown fighters in the Spanish Civil War and told about different countries testing their new warplanes; another had been flying Ford Tri-motors; and others had all kinds of stories to tell.

It was a beautiful December Sunday afternoon in 1936 when Ed Shepard invited me to the terminal for a Coke. It was the day for the big air show, and a very large crowd was outside watching the airplanes do their acrobatics. The restaurant was empty except for the pilots, and soon Shepard got up and left to get ready for his part in the air show. I stayed to listen to the pilots talk flying. We could hear the loud speaker outside talking to the crowd. The announcer called the crowd's attention to Shepard's plane. I got up, went outside, and worked my way through the crowd to the front by the fence. Shepard had a monocoupe, high-wing, green airplane with one door on the right side. He was quite high when he rolled into a vertical dive and then pulled out and started a slow roll. It was then that it looked like his right wing exploded, and the plane started falling in a slow spin.

As soon as I saw the wing break, I jumped over the fence, started running across the airport, and kept watching for his parachute to open. The plane stayed in a very slow spin until it hit the ground in a cotton field just outside the airport boundary. Running up to the crash site was a sight I'll never forget. There was gasoline filling the rows in the cotton field around the small pile of crashed airplane. The engine was driven into the ground, and Ed was smashed flat with his parachute still on. I could see, from what was left of the right wing, that it had folded over the only exit door. He never had a chance to bail out, but he had turned the switch off. That had stopped the engine and prevented a fire.

It was a very strange, weird feeling to be there all alone, just staring at a small pile of wreckage. It seemed like a very long time before anyone arrived, but soon a few people started arriving. Then, without saying a word to anyone, I turned and started walking back to the airport and across the field to the terminal, and then to the hangar. I got my bicycle, and went home. It is hard to describe the complex feeling of a sixteen-year-old who had just watched his friend die in a spectacular crash with hundreds of spectators watching. After being alone at that crash site, I made a resolution to never go to a crash scene, but instead to turn the other way and leave.

Several facts became apparent. First, if a person is going to be in the aviation business, he must be prepared for human losses, because the early days of aviation were dangerous. Second, both the airplane and the pilot have limitations. If either is exceeded, there is great danger. Third, if one is going to be a pilot and have a chance of staying alive, he had better know the aerodynamics of airplanes, and develop very good piloting skills. He might also pray for a little good luck.

Shepard's crash was caused by exceeding the airplane's limitations. When he came out of a vertical dive, he exceeded the maximum G-force (wing load) and compounded this by rolling into a slow roll at a very high speed. The downward right aileron caused a twisting force, resulting in destroying the right wing.

The following summer I asked Kenneth Starnes for a job in his aircraft and engine repair shop located in the hangar at Adams Field. He said he would let me work without pay and learn the aircraft repair business. It was a part of my philosophy of life that if someone knew something I needed to know, and he were willing to teach me, I would gladly work for free until I learned and developed the skill I needed. Besides, just to be in the hangar with all those airplanes was exciting, and the fabric-covered airplanes had a smell that was very pleasant and unique.

Another kid, Bill Miller, worked with me, learning the trade. Mr. Starnes taught us to change, clean, and gap sparkplugs, and how to grind and seat cylinder valves. We disassembled engines for engine overhaul. He taught us how to cover wings and fuselages with fabric, how to rib stitch the fabric, and tape and dope wings. While we didn't make any money, it really paid off throughout our aviation careers. We each ended up holding an aircraft and engine mechanics license, and this contributed greatly to our accident-free pilot skills during our many years as professional pilots.

CHAPTER 2
Civil Pilot Training 1939-1941

The spring of 1939 was high school graduation time, a time when young people start going out into the world on their own, and choosing the path that will lead them into the future. By this time in their lives, they should know where they are going and how they are going to get there. If they don't know where they are going, there is no way they can get there. Also, by this time in a young person's life, his character should be formed, his likes and dislikes should be established, and his philosophy for life should be well- developed. He should be able to see the real world as it is, and not how someone would like it to be, and this would be different for each generation.

When a person devotes eight hours a day to music, as I did in my senior year of high school, he becomes quite accomplished in music. After placing first in the nation in solo French Horn, and with my trophy in the high school trophy case, I began starring as soloist at concerts. I put together a dance band, and being well-trained in conducting band and orchestra, I expected that this would lead to a music career. It did bring in five major scholarships, one of which included a contract to play during opera season. As each university received my transcript, each withdrew their scholarship. That was a bitter lesson. A person cannot spend all his time on one subject and ignore all other subjects. I ended up with a job as assistant bandmaster at Arkansas State Teachers College for my tuition, room and board. After riding the highest high and falling to the lowest low, I knew it was time to face the real world and start studying hard to bring grades up in all subjects.

What was the real world in the spring of 1939? The Japanese had invaded China; Italy had made a hostile conquest of Ethiopia in Africa; and Germany had invaded and annexed Austria, and was taking Czechoslovakia. All this time the world just stood by and did nothing. With their conquests, Germany had become the strongest military power in the world, and with a realistic view, one could only conclude that we were looking at the beginning of World War II. No nation in the world would do anything to stop this aggressive takeover of other nations. This lack of action has always ended with the aggressor becoming more aggressive. By taking a realistic view, I knew I would be involved and would be taking part in the coming war.

Part of my life philosophy was that a person should be doing what he loves doing, and for me that was flying. If given the choice between directing a 120-piece orchestra, which I did, and working in a hangar full of airplanes, which I did, I would choose the hangar. Another part of my life philosophy was always planning my life five years ahead, and it was time for a plan revision. As an old man once said to me, "Tom, if you love flying so much, why don't you join the Army Air Corps? They have a lot of airplanes." The Army Air Corps at that time required a minimum of two years' college. So to meet the college requirement and achieve the goal of joining the Army Air Corps, I attempted to make myself more acceptable by taking engineering courses with lots of math, physics, chemistry and mechanical drawing.

The world situation was very unsettled as I started my freshman year in college. Germany's invasion of Poland caused Great Britain, the Union of South Africa, France, Australia, New Zealand and Canada to declare war on Germany. World War II was then a reality, but few people in our country thought it would affect us. A mass population of peaceniks and isolationists made loud talk and said, "This is not our war." People felt secure because there were two large oceans that separated us from the war. Our college lives were not affected.

In the late fall of 1939, someone in the government somewhere must have realized that to win the coming war, a country had to have the dominant military air power, and our military standing in the world was about seventeenth. So they started a college program to train pilots. It was called the Civilian Pilot Training (CPT) and consisted of ground school and 60 hours in a Piper J-3 Cub with a 50-horsepower engine. Although one year of college was a requirement for the course, my friend and mentor, Kenneth Starnes, had the training contract, and he somehow got me into the first class that was ever offered. What a break it was to be the only freshman to get all the flight training that I had tried so hard to work for during past summers.

The music department, seeing my lack of interest in music, relieved me of the position of assistant bandmaster, and the school then provided the job of washing dishes in the college cafeteria in exchange for tuition, room and board.

The airport was about a mile from the college campus, and I had to walk to and from the airport in order to get a thirty-minute flying lesson. In those days the aircraft engines were not considered reliable. A student could expect the instructor to pull the throttle and yell "Force Landing" at least three times during every thirty-minute lesson. Soon the student didn't have to worry about choosing a place to land the airplane because selecting a field in which to land soon became a subconscious routine that stayed with the pilot all his life. When the instructor cut one's power, the student was expected to instantly pop the stick forward, getting the nose down, and assume glide attitude. They used rectangular patterns, S-turns on a road, and 8's around pylons to teach a pilot to compensate for the crosswind effect. We did medium turns, steep turns, climbing turns and gliding turns to prefect coordination by using the proper rudder pressure. Before our first solo flight we were given approach stalls, power stalls, full oscillation stalls, and two-turn spins. There were many touch-and-go landings, as well as crosswind landings by both slipping and crabbing into wind. Unlike the training today, there was no instrument training. We were taught to fly strictly by the seat of our pants.

Robert R. Ross was my instructor during the Civilian Pilot Training. Some of his first remarks in my logbook were: "Student familiar with theory and mechanics of flight;" "Is familiar with procedures;" "Favorable reaction to flying;" "Shows good natural ability and retains instructions." Ross was an excellent instructor and contributed much to my over 18,000 hours of accident free flying.

There is one day in a pilot's life that he never forgets: the day he makes his first solo flight. He is making full stop landings with his instructor, and just before another takeoff, the instructor gets out of the airplane, and the student is on his own for the first time. The first thing the student notices while taking off, is how fast the plane jumps into the air due to the lighter load. By the time he is turning downwind, he feels the thrill of the occasion, and it's one of the happiest moments in his life. After three takeoff and landings, he taxis back to the hangar, and everyone is there to congratulate him.

Flight training and aviation ground school were complimented by my study of physics, chemistry and mechanical drawing. I not only had gained an understanding of how all of the forces act on an airplane, but I also had learned to calculate the forces. This knowledge helped me to physically feel as if I were part of the plane, such as when the plane was under strain, and I could feel it as though it were a part of my body.

As the freshman year came to a close in late May of 1940, the world situation looked bleaker than ever. Germany had advanced through Europe, and France was defeated and its air force destroyed. The British had lost over half its bombers, and what was left of their army was being evacuated from Dunkirk, France. Churchill replaced Chamberlain as the British Prime Minister, and he assumed the responsibility for victory or defeat. Still, the majority of our population went along with the peaceniks and isolationists. Knowing that war loomed in the near future, I felt my preparation for it should be given top priority, and building flight time was important. As a licensed pilot, I could fly a person anywhere anytime, and all he had to do was rent the airplane. This was a way to build flight time. A few weeks that summer were spent with a crop dusting outfit, doing their aircraft maintenance and service. They did let me ferry aircraft a couple of times, but they would not let me crop dust.

By mid-summer in 1940, the Battle of Britain was in all the newspapers because the Germans were bombing London and other major British cities. The RAF (Royal Air Force), with their Spitfires and Hurricanes fighters, were doing a fantastic job in defense of Britain, but they were losing enough pilots to cause a shortage. Churchill said in one of his famous speeches about RAF pilots: "Never have so many owed so much to so few."

In the fall of 1940 it was back to college for my sophomore year, the year that would complete my educational requirements for the Army Air Corps. Without a scholarship, it was necessary to work and go to college at the same time. Getting a job with the WPA (Works Progress Administration), using a pick and shovel to dig an underground silo for fifteen cents an hour, was the best thing available. There was no leaning on the shovel. It was all hard work, with no rest periods. About the second day on this job, I heard the supervisor say something about building a barn, so I quickly suggested that I should be doing the design and drawings for this new barn. He agreed, and gave me the job of designing and making all the drawings for the new barn. This took care of food and apartment rent for the next three months. Sitting at a drawing board for fifteen cents an hour sure beat the pick and shovel, but after this project I needed another job.

A lady running a boarding house needed a cook, dishwasher and housekeeper. I got the job for room and board. My job was to cook breakfast and do dishes, make beds and sweep floors. It was quite hard to make all of my college classes and find time to study. Knowing this, I spent two or three weeks in the summer before classes started, outlining the coming courses, and I used my Christmas holidays to outline the next semester's classes. The effort produced passing grades. This would take care of all credits needed to receive an associate degree and meet the Army Air Corps requirements.

By January, 1941, with the Battle of Britain and the fall of France, a growing feeling of sympathy for the British was building in America. A noticeable change was taking place. There was very little opposition to increased rearmament and the passing of the Selective Service Act. We had a policy to keep the British supplied with its needs and do everything we could, short of war, to help them. When Britain ran out of cash to buy from us, Congress passed the lend-lease program to help the war effort.

In March of 1941 the government started advanced CPT flight training, and once again, I was in the first class. They used a 220-horsepower open cockpit bi-plane called the Waco UPF-7. The course was primarily 60 hours of acrobatic flying. Acrobatics included loops, chandelles, lazy-eights, snap rolls, barrel rolls, slow rolls, vertical reversals, inverted flight and inverted turns. We also did night flying and night acrobatics.

When the advance flight training started, the job at the boarding house was exchanged for a mechanic job and night watchman at the airport. Aircraft maintenance work would start every night at seven o'clock, and we would finish anywhere from eleven o'clock to one in the morning. After the work was done, I would get in an airplane and sleep until six in the morning. Then I would get the planes out of the hangar and align them on the flight line. At seven the instructors and students would start arriving, and it was time to head for college.

One Sunday, as part of the flight training, I took a cross-country flight in a Waco F-2. This was a hot, good-looking open cockpit biplane, and the highest performing plane I had ever flown. It would take-off and climb at a 45-degree angle and do fantastic acrobatics. Stopping in Searcy, Arkansas, to see some family friends, I saw nearly 1,500 people gathered around a Tri-motor Ford plane. They were selling airplane rides. While taxiing up to park the airplane, I could see them coming over to see the Waco F-2. The crowd was so thick that I was afraid someone would step into the prop, so I quickly cut the engine. Just imagine the high a 20-year-old young, egotistical pilot got as he lifted his goggles up on his leather helmet, got out of the plane, and removed his parachute.

It was only a short walk to where family friends lived, and after a short visit, they drove me back to the plane. My next thought was that what these people needed was a little air show. Getting into the plane, I put my maps on the floor and started the engine. Before people could gather, I took off from a parked position across the grass field, climbing straight out at a 45-degree angle, and then making a tight 180-degree turn to fly back across the field. Nearing the airport and rolling over to fly across the field inverted, the maps that had been lying on the floor started falling past my face. Turning loose of the stick, I tried to grab the maps, but the nose fell, and instead of pushing forward on the stick to raise the nose and doing a half roll, I pulled back on the stick so hard that the G-force was so great that it caused a partial blackout. To this day I do not know how close the plane came to the ground. The lesson well-learned that day was that this was the way young, stupid, egotistical pilots killed themselves, and now this stupid pilot had to find his way home without maps.

With the advance flight training completed and an associate degree in hand, I was off hitchhiking city to city to find a recruiter, and to take exams for the Army Air Corps flight cadet program. After catching up with them and taking a battery of exams, I was interviewed and given a physical exam. They told me; "You'll hear from us in a week or two." It took about a week, and their letter said: "You have been accepted into the Army Air Corps and will receive orders to report soon." Weeks passed without hearing any more from them, and this impatient young man had real doubts about ever receiving orders. The problem was my age, as one had to be 21 to hold a commission, and this delayed the call to report.

The Royal Canadian Air Force was recruiting pilots for the RAF, and serious thought was given to accepting their application. A couple of my pilot friends had already done so. The RAF applications were received and completed twice, and both times pilot friends talked me out of sending the application. Finally, in the latter part of August, 1941, orders came to report to the Army Air Corps Primary Flight School at Thunderbird Field in Phoenix, Arizona. I was to pick up a train ticket at an office in Little Rock, Arkansas. What a thrill it is to successfully achieve one's goal, and suddenly the new goal was to survive the nine months of strenuous cadet training, knowing that on average there was a fifty-percent washout. At the train departure time there were three more men from Little Rock, Arkansas, with orders the same as mine. We were departing on an exciting journey that would forever change our lives. One would washout, and within a year, one would be killed in a plane crash. I never heard of the other pilot again, but it is doubtful that he lived through the war.

CHAPTER 3
Army Air Corps Cadet 1941- 1942

Thunderbird Field in Phoenix, Arizona, was a beautiful and welcome sight after a two-day train ride from Little Rock, Arkansas. We were processed in as the new underclass cadets, and issued uniforms, shoes, bedding and supplies, helmet and goggles. Then, as new underclass cadets, each of us was assigned a room and a roommate. Next there was an orientation lecture, laying out what was expected of us and how we were to live and act. This was the military in its strictest form, and it was made clear that the upperclassmen were in charge.

Promenade, Thunderbird Field

Meals were served in the dining hall on white tablecloths with fine silverware and china. We were assigned to tables that seated six, and there were two or three upperclassmen at each table. Waiters served us at the table. We were expected to use perfect table manners, and if we made a mistake, an upperclassman would order us to finish our meal by eating a square meal. This required the offending cadet to sit at attention and lift a bite of food straight up, and then stop and bring the bite of food straight to his mouth. This is a very hard way to eat, and he was never able to completely relax and eat all his food. We could be sure of one thing: at the end of two weeks, every underclass cadet had perfect table manners and was on his way to becoming an officer and a gentleman.

All flight and ground instructors were civilian, and check pilots were Army Air Corps Officers. In addition to aviation ground school, taught by civilian instructors, we had an extensive study of military strategy and military law, taught by military officers. They spent time teaching the organization of a task force and how it was deployed. We studied military law, including the Articles of War, in great detail. An intelligence briefing was given once a week and this gave us the big worldwide picture of what was happening in the war. It was very surprising to learn that we were, and had been, in a shooting war with Germany in the Atlantic Ocean.

Although our mail was being censored, in a letter to my parents in early September, I stated, "We will be in an open state of war within ninety days." As it turned out, my guess was only off by a week. We all knew that we were going to be fighting, and that they were training us for future air battles, so every cadet was doing his best to prepare for the coming battle.

Meanwhile, cadet life was a living hell. It started at six o'clock every morning with a bugle call on the public address system. In three minutes we had to be dressed and standing in formation on the drill field. When all were present and accounted for, we were off for a one-mile hard run across the airfield and back. Then we were dismissed, and we would run to our rooms to prepare them for room inspection. All underclassmen had to run everywhere they went; that didn't mean "trot;" it had to be a hard run. Only upperclassmen could walk.

It was nearly impossible to meet room inspection requirements. We would come back to our rooms to find our beds unmade, and when we finally did pass inspection, many of us would sleep on the floor, so as to make our beds pass inspection. The upperclassmen soon caught on to this and started making late night check; that put an end to sleeping on the floor. At night when we were trying to study, upperclassmen would barge into our rooms, brace us against the wall, and start shouting in our faces. I became a real target, because as a southern boy, raised and educated in the South, and having a southern accent, I said, "Yessir" instead of "Yes, Sir." It didn't take long before I was talking like a Yankee. Sometimes things were so bad that we wondered if we could take it another five minutes. Some cadets couldn't, and washed out.

Breakfast was served at seven, and we had to be on the flight line or in ground school at eight o'clock. We had one hour a day for calisthenics; during this time we took a two-mile hard run. At first, many of us could not make it, so they told us that at the end of our first two weeks, anyone who couldn't make the run would be washed out. I made it the first time on the last day, but some did not, and they were washed out.

At the end of the first two weeks, we were given "open post" from noon Saturday until 2100 Sunday night. On Saturday night we had a formal dinner and dance with a big band on the top floor of the Westward Hotel in downtown Phoenix. (We called it the Westward Ho House). We were required to dress in our civilian suit, white shirt and tie. We were told that there would be a bar, and that we were welcome to drink, but that anyone who became even slightly intoxicated would be a civilian Monday. That night we lost three cadets.

Tarmac, Thunderbird Field

All flight training was done in an open cockpit biplane with the instructor sitting in the front seat and the student in the back seat. Instructions were communicated through a tube and by way of hand signals. When he wanted to take control of the plane, the instructor would pat the top of his head. There was a mirror mounted on the center section of the upper wing, which allowed us to see each other's face.

E. A. Robert was my instructor in primary training, and the very first flight lesson was one never to be forgotten. He made the takeoff, and then gave me the control. I made a ninety-degree left turn, then a forty-five-degree right turn to leave the traffic pattern. He had me doing turns until we were well within our practice area. Then out of the blue and to my surprise he said, "Do a slow roll." I did a slow roll, and then he said, "I'll try one," and he fell out of it. He was a good pilot and a good flight instructor, but he had no acrobatic training, so we spent all our time doing acrobatics. I had never reported my previous flight experience, but somehow they must have gotten my flight records, because he would never have asked me to do a slow roll if he had not known about my previous training. The student became the teacher until it was time for my twenty- hour check ride, and then he said, "Your twenty-hour check ride is next, so we had better work on that today."

After the check ride, it was back to all acrobatics, and soon we were doing outside spins, outside snap rolls and inverted approaches to landing at a distant practice strip where no one could see us. We kept trying to do outside loops, but when inverted, the gas could not flow to the engine, and with no power, we could only make it about three-quarters' way through the loop. We decided we needed more speed, so we made a plan to start from ten-thousand feet, and when the plane was inverted, we would let the plane build up a high speed; then both of us would push forward on the stick to finish the loop. It didn't work, as we still hit a high velocity stall. I'll never forget the tremendous g-force at the bottom of that outside loop; I could see his face in the mirror. Every blood vessel in his face stood out. If one of our seat belts had broken, when we were only a couple thousand feet from the ground, we would have been unable to open our parachutes before hitting the ground. These maneuvers were not part of the primary flight training.

During the first week or two, when students were being taught turns, if the student failed to look for other aircraft on both sides to see that he was clear of traffic, the instructor would make him do three days of square turns. What is a square turn? As a cadet runs around the base and comes to a turn, he stops, holds his arms outward, looks over and under his right arm, and then over and under his left arm. Then he turns and starts running again. After three days of this, one can be sure this pilot would not make another turn without clearing himself for other aircraft.

After about six weeks, the upperclassmen finished their primary training, and a new class of cadets arrived. Then we were the upperclassmen who had the responsibility of shaping up the new underclassmen. We became the hazer's. To me, dishing it out was almost as unpleasant as being on the receiving end, but it had to be done.

In October of 1941, fifty-three Chinese cadets secretly arrived at Thunderbird Field. They had been training in China, but the Japanese had captured their airfield, and they were brought to Thunderbird Field to finish their flight training. They had their own quarters and their own area to fly in, so there was little mixing with them. At that time we were not at war, and the public did not know about the Chinese at Thunderbird Field.

One day I was flying very near their practice area, and I made a dive on one of them; this started a dogfight. To them, this was a big thing, and after that day I was their friend and would slip over to their quarters and visit. One Chinese cadet could speak very good English; his name was H.C. Chung. He explained, "All the Chinese cadets are officers and graduates of what is like your West Point. We were in flight training in Hangchow, China, when the Japanese bombed and invaded, destroying our flight school. We walked a thousand miles, from Hangchow to Chungking, and then to Kunming. From there we came to the US and to Thunderbird Field."

The weekend of December 6, 1941, was like other weekends: it was "open post", and I went to Phoenix and checked into the San Carlos Hotel. Then I dressed in my Hart-Schaffner & Marks brown suit, white shirt and tie. My date for the evening picked me up at the entrance to the hotel, and we drove a few blocks to the Westward Hotel, took the elevator to the top, and socialized for an hour before the Saturday night banquet. After enjoying a delicious dinner, we walked into the ballroom to enjoy an evening of dancing to the music of a big band orchestra. The Army Air Corps was a great place to be in peacetime.

When the orchestra musicians took a thirty-minute intermission, about eight of our cadets got the OK to use their instruments for a jam session. We had a set of drums and a piano in our recreation room, and once in a while, two or three of us would get together and ham it up a little, but never like this. It was a fantastic show of talent. Everybody gathered around to listen, and even the orchestra musicians were applauding. That night demonstrated what a high quality of men there were in this class. Most had college degrees, all were in perfect health, their character was above question, and it was an honor to be in the same class. The night ended when my date dropped me off at the San Carlos Hotel with the promise to pick me up at eight o'clock the next morning, and we would spend our Sunday together.

The next morning I awoke to find fellow cadets sleeping all over the room. This was how they saved on the cost of hotel rooms. After getting dressed and taking the elevator to the lobby, I could see my date's car at the door. I noticed that a group of people was over by the desk listening to the radio. They were describing the bombing of Pearl Harbor. After listening a few minutes, then getting into my girlfriend's car and turning on the radio, I said, "The Japs have bombed Pearl Harbor. Before long they will be pulling every military man off the street, so let's get out of town because this will be my last open post for a long time." We kept listening to the radio as they kept describing the tremendous damage the Japs had done to our military, and soon we heard, "Attention! All military personnel report to your base immediately." As a cadet, I didn't see that there was anything I could do by returning to Thunderbird Field, so we stopped at a little country place and had a leisurely breakfast.

My thoughts that morning were, that since the nation was so unprepared for war, and since we were already battling Germany on the high seas, and because there was war with Japan, could we win? I had seriously questioned whether or not we could win a war fighting both Germany and Japan. At the best, it could take at least five years. As a military pilot, my chances of living through it were very slim. It is an understatement to say that this was not the happiest day of my life. We spent the day listening to the news on the radio, and later we stopped for me to meet her parents. After dinner, at about nine o'clock, she drove me back to Thunderbird Field.

As we turned into the base, we noticed that there were no lights anywhere. It was in total darkness. As we approached the gate, we saw a soldier appear in the car's headlights. He held a rifle with fixed bayonet pointed straight at us. He ordered me out of the car, and ordered her to turn around and leave. After seeing my ID, he let me proceed to my room in total darkness.

After returning to my room, I slipped over to the Chinese quarters to discover a hilariously happy bunch of Chinese pilots. They kept saying over and over, "Now, you fight with us." Everyone was sitting on the floor, in the dark, talking about it. Then I said, "I think the Japanese act of hara-kiri and committing suicide is stupid." There were a few moments of silence, and then my Chinese friend said, "We believe in the same thing. An important part of our graduation ceremony is the issuing of the hara-kiri dagger." My comeback was, "I still think it is stupid." Little did I realize that before the end of the war, and after finding out what it was like to be taken prisoner by the Japs, my feelings would be more like theirs, though for a different reason. They wanted to honor their ancestors, and I wanted to save one bullet to avoid a slow, painful death.

On Monday morning, December 8, 1941, at Thunderbird Field, things changed drastically. The first order was to pack all civilian clothes and turn them in to be sent home. It would be years before civilian clothes would be worn again. This was our last week at Thunderbird Field, and after a brief talk by the officer in charge of the base, we were given orders sending us to basic training. My orders read: "Proceed by train to Minter Field at Bakersfield, California."

Several of us boarded the train in Phoenix for the trip to Bakersfield on December 15, 1942. All the war news was bad. The U.S. and Britain had declared war on Japan and Germany. Germany and Italy had declared war on the U.S. China officially declared war on Japan and Germany. Japan sank two major British warships, the Prince of Wales and the Repulse. Japan captured the island of Guam and attacked Burma and Wake Island. To make matters worse, the United States was bracing for the Japanese to attack on our West Coast, and the coastal area was blacked out. The results of being unprepared for war were very apparent, and there was nothing that would give us any confidence of a successful outcome of the war, except the very determined spirit of the military and the public. The military recruiting offices were crowded with very long lines of men volunteering for duty, and many young men were lying about their age; the recruiters were not questioning them. Still others had written permission from their parents.

On reporting in at my new air base at Minter Field, the first thing I learned was that two upper-class cadets had been killed the previous week while night flying. One had been on a local solo night flight, and the other was killed during a solo night cross-country flight. We were told that it was caused by spatial disorientation due to night blindness. This is a condition wherein, with the absence of any horizontal reference, the pilot's inner ear sensors tell him that he is making a hard turn, when in reality, he is not. The inexperienced pilot will react by making a hard turn opposite to what his inner ear sensors are telling him, and he will end up in what is called "The Death Spiral". This is a tight downward spiral that ends in a crash. With proper training and experience, a pilot will learn to ignore his sensors and believe his instruments.

There was a big difference between Thunderbird Field and Minter Field. Thunderbird was beautiful with well-kept grounds, and Minter was plain with two-story military barracks. Thunderbird had all civilian instructors, and Minter had only military instructors, with no civilians involved. Thunderbird had formal dining, but Minter had typical GI mess. At Minter Field there was much more marching; life was very military.

BT-13 Valiant

In basic flight training we logged about eighty hours in a BT-13, with a 450 horsepower Pratt and Whitney engine. We were taught formation flying and night flying, both local and cross-country. Our night cross-country was from Bakersfield to Flagstaff, Arizona. This was on the old low frequency range airway called "Green Six". There were rotating beacons every ten or fifteen miles, and they had a red light flashing a Morse code indemnifier. A white and green flashing beacon identified an airport.

Instrument training was accomplished by putting the student under a hood, and flying using only the needle, ball and airspeed. Artificial horizons were not considered reliable in those days. At a high degree of bank or pitch, the artificial horizon would tumble, and the needle ball wouldn't tumble; therefore, we had to learn to do all our instrument flying using those instruments. It was needle, ball and airspeed. We were also taught to correct for the lead and lag of the magnetic compass on north and south headings.

We had flight check rides after twenty hours, and it came as a shock when I learned that I had failed the check ride. There would be one more check ride, and failing the second check ride would make me a civilian the next day. They said that I didn't use enough rudders, but, with by far more flight time and training than some of the instructors, that wasn't true. The problem was my egotistical attitude, and they corrected that very quickly.

All further check rides went smoothly with no problems, and by the middle of February, 1942, the eighty hours of flight time in the BT-13's were completed. With orders in hand, I was off by train to Luke Field in Phoenix, Arizona, for advanced flight training.

While we were in basic training, our country continued losing the war. Wake Island was lost to the Japanese, and the fall of Rangoon, Burma, caused the loss of the last supply route to China over the Burma Road. Singapore fell to the Japanese, and fifty- thousand British, Australian, and Indian troops were taken prisoner, only to be used as forced labor in jungles. A high percentage would die due to malnutrition, execution, and diseases. So far, we were losing the war with Japan. On the German front, Russia was losing its war, and the Germans and Italians were winning big victories in North Africa. On the home front, gasoline and some foods were being rationed. Our industries and the country's manpower were being mobilized.

AT-6 formation near Luke Field

Luke Field was different. Advanced training was all about fighter pilot training in AT-6's, with a thirty-caliber machine-gun firing through the propeller. It had a six- hundred horsepower engine, constant speed propeller, and a retractable landing gear. Like the BT-13, the student sat in the front, and the instructor sat in the backseat. It was a fun plane to fly and great for acrobatics.

The instructors were all military, and each instructor had five students. After the instructor had checked out all his students, he had us do a lot of formation flying. He taught his students how to takeoff and gather into a formation. Before long we were making formation takeoffs. He taught us how to fly in a "V" and echelon formations, and make timed break-offs for landings. Instrument flight training, under the hood in the airplane and in a Link Trainer, was taught using the Low Frequency Range System for navigation and instrument approaches.

A Low Frequency Range Station had four quadrants: two quadrants of the Morse Code A (dot dash), and two quadrants of N (dash dot). At the intersection of each quadrant, the A and N tones came together to make a continuous tone, called the "beam". The airways were made up of a string of Low Frequency Range Stations, and we would fly the airway route by flying on the beam from one station to another. Directly over the station was a cone of silence, and with our ADF (Automatic Direction Finder) tuned to the station frequency, the needle on the ADF would turn 180 degrees as we passed the station.

For instrument approaches, the station on course beam was aligned with the instrument runway and three or four miles from the approach end of the runway. Holding patterns were on the out-bound beam. We made instrument approaches by leaving the station outbound at high cone altitude and descending to procedure turn altitude. After completing the procedure turn, we descended to minimum low cone altitude. After passing low cone, we timed our descent to minimum instrument approach altitude. At minimum instrument approach altitude, if we could not see the runway, we followed the missed approach procedure.

In ground school, a lot of time was spent studying both German and Japanese aircraft. We also studied how to recognize them and where to put a bullet so it would do the most good. The RAF (Royal Air Force) aerial combat experience was being sent to us. This information proved very valuable and was used to show where it was best to place our bullets, and what maneuvers worked, and what maneuvers didn't work in aerial combat.

Life at Luke Field was pure military. We were taught the care and use of the rifle, the 45-caliber pistol, and the 12-gauge shotgun. On the rifle and pistol ranges we had to qualify in marksmanship, and we spent hours shooting skeet to learn how to lead a moving target. We had to learn to adjust fighter wing guns to converge on a point at a distance in front of the aircraft. The individual pilot selects the point of convergence. He determines how close he wants to get to the target before firing his guns. The closer the pilot gets to his target, the more fire power he has to damage the enemy, but the more chance of damage he can experience to his aircraft from flying debris.

A few weeks were used to teach aerial gunnery, and one could not believe how much ammunition we used in shooting at ground targets and the aerial tow targets. To determine one's score, the bullets were colored, so one's hits could be counted by the color of the bullet hole. About every fifth bullet was a tracer bullet, and this would let us see the path of our bullet. The aerial tow target was a white windsock towed on a long cable by an AT-6 with an observer sitting backwards in the rear seat. We made our approach at about ninety degrees to the path of the target, and both ground and aerial targets had a foul line, a point at which firing had to stop. If we fired beyond the foul line, our score was reduced. When the scores were counted, mine was the third highest in a class of fifty-seven. Surely, this would guarantee me a fighter pilot assignment, which I desperately wanted. Shooting at tow targets, ground targets and sagebrush was getting boring, and we were all ready to get a real live enemy aircraft in our gun sight.

Curtiss P-36 Hawk

A few cadets were given the opportunity to fly a real fighter plane. It was a Curtiss-Wright P-36, powered by a Pratt & Whitney twelve-hundred horsepower engine with a speed of over three-hundred miles per hour. What a thrill it was to fly, and I was lucky to get over eight hours in that aircraft.

One day our instructor had all five of his students doing formation flying. He was leading us in an echelon formation, and I was in the number six position. My good friend, Bob Heinz, was in the number five position. The instructor radioed instructions to break at thirty-second intervals ninety degrees to the right, and form a string. When it was Bob's turn to break, the instructor was so far away that he was just a dot in the sky, flying directly away from us. So I broke with Bob, added power, climbed a little, and then dived down and did a slow roll around his plane. I'll never forget seeing his head follow me as I passed over the top of his aircraft. So I pulled up and did two rolls around him. Suddenly, looking ahead, I could see that the instructor had made a ninety-degree turn and was rocking his wings, which was the signal to reform the formation. After another ninety-degree turn, we each fell in to form another echelon formation heading straight to Luke Field.

On the downwind leg of the traffic pattern, we turned base leg at thirty-second intervals, and one by one landed, and then taxied to parking. The instructor was first to reach the parking ramp, and I was the last. Taxiing up to park, I saw him running toward my plane, and before I could lock the brake, he was on my wing with his head in the cockpit screaming, "You will be a civilian tomorrow." It was only a week before graduation, and I was going to get washed out.

The next morning I called American Airlines, and after hearing the whole story, they promised me an airline pilot job over the phone. The next day went by, and no one said anything about the flying incident, so I didn't ask anyone. A week passed, and nothing was said. Twenty years would pass before the truth would be known.

Barry Goldwater was serving as our physical training instructor while he was waiting for a commission in the US Army Air Corps. He was a seasoned pilot and had his schooling at the Staunton Military Academy. Twenty years later, he was a US Senator from Arizona and was to be the speaker at a political meeting in Wyoming. He was to fly into Billings, Montana, visit with my family, and I would fly him to

Wyoming and then on to Denver. There he would take an airline back to Washington, D C.

Major Barry Goldwater

When he arrived in Billings, Montana, there was such a large crowd in the terminal that it took 45 minutes to get to a private room for a meeting with the governor of Montana. That meeting lasted only a few minutes, and then my wife, son, daughter and I got to visit about an hour with him before we took-off for Wyoming. There must have been 3,000 people at the meeting, and I watched him shake hands with most of them. After the meeting we went to our motel room. There was a fifth of Old Crow on the night stand between our two beds. Old Crow and water, with no ice, was Goldwater's favorite drink. It was like old times in Karachi, India, when he was liaison officer for Crescent Airline, and I was establishing the CBI portion of the Rocket Airline. (Both were military airlines.) Every afternoon, after 5 o'clock, we would sit in chairs, in front of our basha, and drink Barry's Old Crow with warm water. There was no ice in India.

In Wyoming that night, we were discussing everything from politics to our CBI experiences, when all of a sudden he said, "Damn it! I saved your military career." I asked, "What do you mean, you saved my military career?" He said, "I was at your hearing. They were going to wash you out, and I stood up and told them that any pilot that can do slow rolls around another airplane, is a pilot we need in this war." After twenty years, this was the first time I knew there had been a hearing, much less what was said.

The next day we flew to Denver and had a passenger, who had just returned from a meeting in Chicago. He was there to tell Goldwater that he would be nominated as the Republican Candidate for the President of the United States. I don't think he was too happy to hear this, and it came as a surprise. His entire effort was to bring Conservatives into the party and get the Liberals out.

April 24, 1942, was graduation day for the Army Air Corps Class of 42-D. That morning, about 0900, three C-47 transport planes landed and taxied to the ramp. At 1000 the graduation ceremony took place, and we were all made 2nd Lieutenants and given Army Air Corps Wings to wear. Then we were handed our orders. At 1200 there were a lot of weddings that took place, and at 1500 the three C-47's were loaded; they took-off for we knew not where. However, a few weeks later one of my classmates' picture showed up in Life Magazine. He had shot down his first Japanese enemy plane a week after graduation.

My orders read: "Proceed by train to Victorville Army Air Base in Victorville, California." What a blow! My heart was set on combat and flying fighters, but I would be training bombardiers flying Beechcraft AT-11's. After all, I had placed near the top of the class in aerial gunnery and had checked out in a real fighter aircraft. One would think they would select the most qualified for a fighter pilot job, but no; the army had just blocked off an alphabetical list. Heinz, Heller and I, as well as other pilots whose name started with an "H", were sent to train bombardiers in the Mojave Desert. With all our fighter training, we were learning that there was a right way and then there was the Army way.

While we were at Luke Field, we knew that the war was still being lost. In the Philippines, Bataan had fallen, and Rangoon, Burma, had been taken. The Japanese were driving north against the British, closing the Burma Road, which was China's last supply route. The only bright spot in the news was the bombing of Japan by Doolittle's 16 B-25's. This gave a big morale boost to the population, but much time would pass before people would know the whole story.

Lt. Thomas Herrod

CHAPTER 4
Victorville Army Air Base 1942

I was a very proud new Army Air Corps officer who arrived on a Friday at Victorville Army Air Base. In full dress with new Class A Uniform, with gold 2nd Lieutenant bars on the shoulders, and wearing new silver wings pinned on the blouse, I reported for duty. The first thing said was, "Weekend leaves for all 2nd Lieutenants have been cancelled; all 2nd Lieutenants will report at the drill field at 0800 in the morning, and you can expect to spend the day drilling. Yesterday the commanding officer came driving into the base, and two airmen failed to salute his car, even when his car properly displayed his rank." Would anyone believe that on the first day on duty, the first thing I learned about the Army that day was that there was no rank or grade in the Army lower than a 2nd Lieutenant? If some GI broke the rules, who got punished? They would be the 2nd Lieutenants. Who would be held responsible for shaping up the base discipline? They would be the 2nd Lieutenants. Therefore, the air base was quickly shaped up, and our right arms got plenty of exercise saluting, just while we were walking from the BOQ (Bachelor Officer's Quarters) to the flight line.

AT-11 near Victorville

Victorville Army Air Base was used for training bombardiers to use the Norden Bombsight. The Norden Bombsight at that time was one of the nation's top military secrets, and it was impressive to see the security that was used to protect that secret. The air base was in the Mojave Desert. That was the perfect place for locating bomb targets, which were large circles that had a center marker to serve as the target. Desert could be seen in all directions except when looking to the southwest was where the San Bernardino mountain range was. There were several very large dry lakebeds on which an airplane could land.

Before we could start flying with bombardier cadets, we had to go to class on the Norden Bombsight and qualify on a bombsight simulator. The classroom was a one-room building surrounded by a high security fence; it was under heavy guard while classes were taking place. While attending a class, sitting at our desks, we were allowed no pencils or paper, and our hands had to be on top of the desks. The officer giving the lecture would use blackboards that covered two sides of the classroom. When he completed his lecture, he had us sit at our desks while two men came into the classroom and scrubbed the blackboards with soap and water.

The Norden Bombsight was a wonderful piece of equipment, and living with the knowledge of how the top-secret bombsight was built and operated, had a profound effect on us, especially when we were off the base. We were constantly aware and suspicious of people around us. Whenever we would have a drink in the lounge at the San Bernardino Hotel, we were very careful about how much we drank, and we never became even slightly intoxicated. In a couple of months all the security would be dropped, as the Germans and Japanese had captured the bombsight from wrecked aircraft, which had been lost due to enemy fire.

The bombsight simulators were located in a large hangar-like building. The floor was covered with a scaled picture of the earth's surface, as it would appear to a pilot flying several thousand feet above the ground. The bombsight, with all the bombardier instruments and switches, was located on an elevated platform that moved over the floor. An instructor controlled the bombsight simulator's travel over the floor to set up a bomb run, but once on a bomb run, the bombsight controlled the travel of the platform. It was quite sophisticated, as it was like the real bombardier's compartment, and the bombsight would adjust for airspeed and crosswinds.

The aircraft used for bombardier training was the Twin Beechcraft D-18, modified with a bombardier compartment in the glass nose, and bomb racks with Bombay doors on either side of a catwalk behind the pilot's seat. The bomb racks held ten one-hundred-pound bombs. There were five bombs on either side of the center catwalk. We used practice bombs, which were the same size as a real one-hundred-pound bomb, and fused like a real bomb. They exploded on impact and produced a lot of black smoke.

During one of my first days at Victorville, while standing on the flight line about 1700, the sky was suddenly filled with aircraft coming in to land at Victorville. The West Coast was expecting a Japanese attack, and all unneeded military aircraft were evacuating the West Coast area. Right where I was standing, three giant four-engine aircraft taxied up and parked. Those were the biggest airplanes that I had ever seen. They all had yarn strings stuck all over to the wing and fuselage; these were used to observe and photograph the airflow over their surfaces. The planes must have been newly developed aircraft undergoing flight-tests. They eventually became the Douglas C-54's, and after the war they became known on the airlines as the Douglas DC-4's.

Two civilian pilots arrived at Victorville about the same time, and they were waiting to be commissioned as service pilots. The military needed pilots and was offering a commission to civilian commercial pilots. These two had been employed as test pilots for Consolidated Aircraft Company, but since the war had started, they had been delivering aircraft to Hawaii and flying PBY's back. Getting acquainted with these two pilots was a lucky break, as one of them agreed to give me my first multiengine training.

They both had had some very interesting experiences. One told about a Japanese Sub shooting at him during the night, while he was returning in a PBY from Hawaii to Los Angeles. The other told about returning to the West Coast with a ship's navigator on his first airplane trip. During the night he asked the navigator to take a fix and give him an ETA (estimated time of arrival) for the West Coast. It normally took no more than twenty minutes to take a three-star fix and determine an ETA. After forty-five minutes he went back to see why the navigator had not given him an ETA. He found the ship navigator having a leisurely dinner, and the navigator told him that he would get the ETA after he finished eating. Having no faith in the navigator, he radioed his own ETA. The West Coast at night was under blackout, and at the navigator's ETA, searchlights lit up his PBY, and he received some antiaircraft fire. A quick radio call stopped the shooting. It turned out that he had been wrong, and that the old ship navigator's ETA was right, even if it had been his first airplane flight. Later, these two came to Victorville and were given Captains' commissions.

What a lucky break it was to have an experienced test pilot teach me all about twin engine flying in an AT-11, which was a twin Beechcraft D-18 powered by two four- hundred-and-fifty horsepower R-985 Pratt and Whitney engines, and which had a cruise speed of about one-hundred-and-eighty miles per hour. During the check-out, we went through all the emergency procedures, including engine-out procedures. He also taught me how to determine the minimum engine-out controllable speed. We landed on one of the dry lakebeds; he got out of the plane and with the heel of his shoe, he drew a line. Getting back into the plane, he proceeded to teach me to taxi without the use of brakes, and to end up stopped on the line. During night instrument training, he had me descend at five-hundred feet per minute until we touched down on a very large, dry lakebed. This was rather scary, as when we hit the dry lakebed, we were thrown forward, and the tail rose, pinning the airplane to the ground. This dry lakebed later became Edwards Air Force Base. The things this test pilot taught me contributed to years of accident-free flying, and were used to teach others during many hours of flight instruction.

The bombardier cadets were all washout flying cadets and a wonderful group of men to work with. They were all well-educated, in perfect health, well-trained in military discipline, and highly motivated. On each training flight, we would take two cadets, and each would get to drop five bombs. Each flight started by the cadets checking out a Norden bombsight from a well-guarded vault, and then bringing it to the airplane and mounting it in the bombsight holder located in the bombardier's compartment. Meanwhile, at the operations office, the pilot was assigned a set of targets and an altitude at which to fly. With everything ready, we would takeoff and climb to our assigned altitude, while heading toward the first target.

Next, we would line up on the first target, and when the pilot had the target insight, the pilot would turn control of the airplane over to the bombardier, who controlled the bombsight. The bombardier would keep the crosshairs on the target by adjusting the bombsight settings. The vertical crosshair line would correct for wind drift, and the horizontal crosshair would adjust for speed and altitude, and determine when to automatically release the bomb. When the bomb dropped from the bomb rack and out of the airplane, the bombardier would holler, "Bombs Away", and the pilot would once again have control of the airplane.

During the spring and summer of 1942, there was a great amount of pressure on us to get these men trained and ready for combat. We were flying day and night, and much of the time we were at sixteen-thousand feet and on oxygen. Some pilots were experiencing the bends. The bends is a result of pressure changes that causes nitrogen to form in the joints, and it is painful. During the week we were logging hours fast, but on Saturday and Sunday, we could go into town or take one of the AT-11's and fly anywhere we wanted. One weekend Bob Heinz and I flew from Victorville to Denver, spent the night, and returned by way of Salt Lake City. It was on this trip, and when approaching Winslow, Arizona, that I could see the large meteor crater just ahead of us. I got up and left the cockpit to use the relief tube in the back of the airplane. Bob dove the plane down into the crater, and then up and out the other side. Being in the back of the plane, I missed seeing a close-up of this famous meteor crater.

One day, shortly after arriving in Victorville, an officer came down the hall of the BOQ yelling, "Anybody want to buy a car?" I asked, "What you got?" He came into my room and pointed out the window at a 1932 Ford Roadster. I asked, "How much?" He answered, "Seventy-five dollars." I handed him seventy-five dollars, and he handed me the keys. It was my first car. It provided weekend transportation to San Bernardino, Los Angeles, Long Beach and Big Bear Lake. We were living it up with the candle burning at both ends. I rented a room in Victorville for one month, and when I moved out, the landlady said, "I don't understand you. You rented the room for a month, spent three nights in it, and each time you slept twenty-four hours." Only a twenty-one-year old could fly all day and party all night.

There was one night that will never be forgotten. A very large forest fire was burning in the San Bernardino Mountains. With all the smoke, there was no visibility, and we were flying west trying to find our targets. Suddenly, we broke out of the smoke, and three searchlights hit us. We were on the west side of the San Bernardino Mountain Range. Remembering what had happened to my test pilot friend, when the searchlights had hit his PBY, I made a steep one-hundred-and-eighty degree turn, and we headed east back to Victorville, landing with our full load of bombs.

By the end of the first five months of war with Japan, all battles had been lost, and the only bright thing was Doolittle's B-25's bombing of Japan. In May of 1942, we saw the surrender of Mandalay and Corregidor. The Navy battle in the Coral Sea was a draw. In June, the Japanese attacked and occupied the Aleutian Islands. The Battle of Midway was not only the biggest naval battle in Navy history, but it also was the turning point in the war with Japan. During this period, the war in the European Theater was not doing well; while bombing raids were increasing in size, the advances by Germany and Italy in North Africa were threatening Egypt and the Suez Canal. The German U-boats were sinking a very high number of supply ships in the Atlantic and along the East Coast of the United States. With everything taking place in the world, the people of our nation were united and dedicated to the task of defeating Germany, Italy, and Japan. It truly was the Greatest Generation, and only with these kinds of free people, could our nation survive.

When a class of cadets completed their bombardier training and were commissioned 2nd Lieutenants, a new class of cadets would arrive. The Army Air Corps had been forced to lower the standards, and the majority of the new cadets only had a high school education. They were a difficult group to work with, and one day while on a bomb run, the bomb failed to release. The problem was due to the bomb not having been placed on its rack properly. One of the cadets went back to correct the problem, and one stayed in the bombardier's compartment. As one cadet was standing on the narrow catwalk with the Bombay doors open, lifting the one-hundred pound bomb, trying to get it on the rack, the other cadet hit the switch releasing the bomb into his arms. He was off balance and could not hold on. Finally he let go of the bomb. It fell through the Bombay doors, and I thought the cadet was going to fall out, also. It was starting to become a comedy of errors.

With this class, we started getting a lot of dry runs. A dry run is a bomb run when the bomb fails to drop, because the cadet has failed to have everything set right. It was very early one morning in August on a training flight, when two cadets gave me ten dry runs. They just did not know the bombardier's switches and controls. At the end of the flight, I told them to stay in the airplane and learn the location of all the switches and controls. Then I was assigned another flight. After finishing my flight, I was ordered to report to the CO, at the base headquarters. He gave me hell for leaving those two cadets in the airplane on a hot August day in the middle of the Mojave Desert.

It seemed that every four months I had to screw up. First, it was flunking the twenty-hour check ride while in basic training; second, it was doing slow rolls around another airplane in advance training. Now here I went again. I said to my CO, "If this is the way you are going to run your base, you can send me to combat." That did it! He ordered me out of his office, and in less than fifteen minutes I had orders in my hand, sending me to a combat unit at Columbia, South Carolina. This was a medium bomber base flying B-25's and forming new bomb groups.

My orders read to travel by train, and the route took me through Little Rock, Arkansas. This afforded me the opportunity to spend a few days with my family. It had been a year since leaving Little Rock, yet it seemed so long ago. So much had happened in that year.

That night, the train departed Victorville at 2100, and I had an upper berth in the Pullman car. While waiting for the Pullman car to be converted to a sleeping car, I went forward to the coach car and sat down beside a beautiful young lady. We had a very nice visit, and I offered to share my upper berth with her. She accepted, and we went back to the Pullman car. As I was lifting her up into the upper berth, the conductor came through the Pullman car and changed our plans. He escorted her back to the coach car and sent the Pullman porter with a ladder that made getting into the upper berth easy. It is a gross understatement to say, "It had not been a good day," but the lesson learned that day was "Always ask for a lower berth."

CHAPTER 5
Columbia Army Air Base 1942

My train rolled into Little Rock, Arkansas, and my family was there to meet me. One year had passed since leaving for Army Air Corps pilot training, and so much had changed... so much had happened. The country had changed from peace to total war. Everywhere anyone looked, he would see military uniforms. Gasoline and some foods were rationed. To save gasoline and rubber tires, we had to observe a thirty-five-mile-per- hour national speed limit. Nowhere could one find an isolationist or a peacenik; the entire population was completely dedicated to winning the war.

During the few days at home, I found time for a visit with my old college physics teacher, to thank him for a job well-done. He asked me to speak to his class. It was a pleasure to explain how everything learned in his class had applied to the field of aviation, how it had made me a much better pilot, and how it would also help them in whatever field of work they chose.

I'll never forget my departure from home. When it was time for me to leave for Columbia, South Carolina, everybody was cheerful, except Aunt Rose, and she couldn't stop crying. Readers will be interested to know that Aunt Rose was our colored maid, but she was more of a loving nanny than a maid. She had been a part of the family as far back as I could remember. She and her family were our responsibility, and we were her responsibility. If someone in her family was sick, my mother was at their home, helping to take care of them. Before we had our Thanksgiving or Christmas dinner, we would take dinner to her family. I remember attending a funeral for one of her family members. We went to their church for the funeral, but because of segregation, we sat on the last row in the church. That was the way it was done in those days, but we were reared to respect and care for them. Maybe Aunt Rose was the only one that day who could clearly see that my chances of making it through the war alive were quite small. I have never forgotten the emotion she showed.

The Columbia Air Base was typically military, with its runways and a tarmac. Operation buildings were located along the tarmac and taxiways, through the woods leading to many revetments, each of which held a B-25. The office buildings and barracks had no insulation, but all had potbelly coal-burning stoves. There was a lot of flying, as B-25 training was going on day and night. As soon as enough crews were trained, a new medium bomb group would be formed and sent to combat.

North American B-25

During the month of September in 1942, fifty-one airmen were killed, in groups of two and three, in B-25 crashes at the Columbia Airbase. It seemed as if every time we looked, we saw another cloud of black smoke rising from another crash. Two crashes were on the airfield. While an engine-out landing was being made, the pilots decided to abort the landing and go around. Both were below engine-out controllable speed. One crash was gruesome. The plane crashed in front of a crowd, which had been watching on the tarmac, and the decapitated head of one of the pilots rolled in front of the observers.

After reporting for duty at Columbia Air Base, I started studying the tech manuals on the B-25B, and I spent a few hours sitting in the pilot's seat, learning the cockpit switches and controls. This really paid off during my first flight in a B-25 as copilot with a newly checked-out pilot. We were shooting night touch-and-go landings. The pilot kept complaining about how tired he was, so after two or three landings, I said, "Why don't you let me fly, and you rest?" He did, so we changed seats, and for the next two hours I shot touch-and-go landings. He never knew, and I never told him, that this had been my first flight in a B-25, and my first experience with a tricycle landing gear.

With all my multiengine experience and the benefit of the training received from one of the test pilots while at Victorville, I wanted to find the B-25's engine-out controllable speed. It was obvious that the pilots had been letting the plane get below engine-out controllable speed, and that that had been causing most of the fatal crashes. A pilot determines the engine-out controllable speed by setting one engine to zero thrust and starting to slow the aircraft down. He will finally reach a speed below which he can no longer maintain directional control. While determining the engine-out controllable speed, I found that the pilot needed help to apply enough rudder force to maintain directional control. I always had the copilot keep his feet on the rudders during takeoff and be ready to apply rudder pressure in the event of engine failure at slower speeds during takeoff. Once the plane exceeded a one-hundred-and-thirty-mile-per-hour indicated airspeed, the copilot could remove his feet from the rudders. If someone had made the pilots aware of these aeronautical facts, many lives may have been saved.

After being checked out on the B-25, I was made a B-25 flight instructor. One day on an instrument training flight with the student under the hood, I was getting bored and wanted a chance to operate the fifty-caliber gun turrets. Putting a very qualified flight engineer in the copilot seat to look out for other aircraft, I went to the rear of the plane to play with the guns. Climbing into the top twin fifty-caliber gun turret, I was playing combat by aiming at every passing aircraft. This was a safe thing to do because there was no ammunition aboard the aircraft. Next, I lowered the bottom gun turret down and started playing with it until smoke came from one of the electric motors, and the turret stopped operating. This was no problem since one only had to use the hand crank to raise the gun turret. However, there was no hand crank aboard the aircraft, and the tech manual made it clear that a pilot couldn't land the aircraft with the turret down and the guns extended. Suddenly, I had a problem, so I called the tower declaring an emergency.

After circling the field for the next hour, the fuel supply was running low, and there was no solution to the problem. Everybody assumed that the airplane would be severely damaged on landing. The emergency crew was put into place by the runway, and a crowd had gathered on the tarmac to watch the landing. By making a long final approach with full flaps, landing with a much higher than normal landing speed, and applying steady braking to keeping the tail as high as possible, I brought the plane to a stop without either of the two guns touching the runway. Armament personnel came aboard with a hand crank and raised the bottom turret, after which we taxied to the revetment, followed by a string of vehicles.

Everybody wanted to know how one could land a B-25 with the bottom turret down and the guns extended. This twenty-one-year-old second lieutenant pilot was feeling like a hero and explaining all the details, when a staff car drove into the revetment. The Sergeant driver said, "The colonel wants to see you." As I sat down in the staff car, I thought: "My Commanding Officer wants to know how it was done also; this is turning out to be a great day."

At group headquarters I was ushered into the CO's office. Standing before him at attention, I saluted, and he returned the salute without looking up. Then he handed me a paper to read. It was my promotion to first lieutenant. I laid it back on his desk and thought: "What a great day it was turning out to be." The colonel stopped what he was doing, picked up my promotion letter, and tore it into about six pieces. I knew immediately something was wrong. He started chewing me out like no one had ever done before. Once more I experienced going from the highest emotional high to the lowest emotional low. He said, "You were the pilot in command of that aircraft with a student under the hood. You left the cockpit to go back to play with the guns. Then, you burned a motor up, and for that you are going to buy a gun turret at a cost of fifteen- hundred dollars to be deducted from your pay." I said, "Sir, I had a motor burn out and didn't damage the gun turret." Still standing at attention, I took one step backward, saluted, turned, and left his office. In those few minutes I not only lost my promotion to 1st Lieutenant, but I also found myself fifteen-hundred-dollars in debt.

I passed the Sergeant Major's desk as he called, "Lieutenant Herrod." To my surprise he was a fellow I had known at home, before the war, and he had something to say. "There is a new combat group being formed, and I can get you transferred into it. It will get you out of here tonight. With your experience you could have made squadron CO, but all those positions are filled. The best I can do is a job as squadron flight leader, which isn't bad since it supports a position of

Major, and it will get you out of this mess." Without one second of hesitation, I accepted the position.

The transfer was to the 340th bomb group, and I was squadron flight leader of the 486th bomb squadron. I was given a B-25C and a new crew. The crew of seven consisted of a pilot, copilot, navigator, bombardier, flight engineer and two gunners. The training was intense with a lot of formation work, bombing and gunnery practice. They encouraged us to get a lot of cross-country trips to any place we wanted to fly. On some flights I would let the crew pick trips to their hometowns to see their parents and RON (remain over night), so the crew could go out on the town.

One crewmember's home was in Dayton, Ohio, so on October 7, 1942; we ended up landing at Wright Patterson Airbase about 1500 in the afternoon. (For years this was the aeronautical research and test center for new aircraft.) After landing, we taxied to the transit parking area. It was just in front of the control tower, which was located on the corner of a large hangar where the operations office was located.

I'll never forget that afternoon while sitting in the cockpit, looking out at all the newly developed aircraft that were there to be test-flown. There were all types of aircraft parked in front of us. One was a very large four-engine bomber; some were new twin-engine bombers; and several were fighter type aircraft. While still sitting in the cockpit, I observed a short distance in front of us, something came up vertically and flew around backwards, sideways, and forward, and finally descended vertically to land. I would later learn that it was called a "helicopter", and it had been the first one any of us had ever seen.

When reporting at the operations office, I asked the operation officer, "Do you have someone who could show me all these aircraft?" He picked up the phone and called someone. An officer came out of an office adjoining the operations office, and introduced himself. The crew had left in a hurry to get to town, leaving me to take a guided tour of all those airplanes.

The first airplane he showed me was a very large four-engine bomber. While inside this very large airplane, we walked out into the right wing. The officer opened a door, and we were looking at the rear of the number- three engine. A person could have also gone out in the wing to the number- four engine. This was a big airplane, but it was never put into production. He spent over an hour showing me different airplanes, and then he said, "Come on into my office; I want to show you something."

Once inside his office, he closed the door, walked over to a wall, and raised a large curtain, behind which were data and charts. He said, "We believe there is a problem when an airplane's speed reaches the speed of sound. We believe that at that point, the air molecules can no longer warn other molecules that the wing is coming, and that this causes a wave of air vibrations that causes damage to the wings. About a week ago we were doing a terminal dive in a new fighter plane when it came apart. The pilot got out but was badly injured. He lived long enough to describe what he had seen as the wings were coming apart. We have a new plane that we feel is strong enough to cross over this barrier. It's a new single-engine fighter, and we have installed a full feathering prop, and have mounted two rockets on it that should create enough power to get past this barrier." He then pointed to the power curve chart on the wall and said, "This is the power you will have and the speed that you will reach. As you can see on this chart, once you pass the speed of sound, the power required will drop back, and you can see the expected speeds you will reach. We need a pilot to volunteer to take it up to its service ceiling, feather the prop, and fire the rockets. These charts represent the power curve and performance that we expect with this rocket power. We need a pilot to volunteer to fly this test. Would you volunteer?"

My answer was, "Thanks, but no thanks," explaining that as squadron flight leader in a B-25 group that was getting ready to be deployed, I would not feel right leaving the group. By this time it was after 1800, and after thanking him again for the tour, I asked the operations officer to get me transportation to a hotel downtown.

At that late hour there were no rooms left, and no member of my crew could be found; they were all out on the town. After checking my B-4 bag with the desk clerk, I started down the street and came to a dance hall. Thinking that someone in this dance hall should have a place for this service man to sleep, I asked one of the many young ladies to dance. Once on the dance floor, I planned to explain my problem and how tired I was. After about three or four different dance partners, one dancing partner said, "I've got a room at the hotel and would be glad to share it with you." Since I wanted to get some rest, but she wanted to dance, I took her key, and I promised to leave the door unlocked. That was the last time I ever saw her.

The next morning, transportation to the airport was at the hotel. After the pre-flight procedures, we took off, and made another cross-country training flight, ending the day back at the Columbia Army Air Base. At least I was given the opportunity to be the first pilot to break the sound barrier. Of course, we will never know who actually flew that rocket-powered aircraft. Today, we do know that neither the aircraft nor the pilot could have survived. That was another experience that can be called "cheating death again".

We were doing a lot of low-level skip bombing and treetop cross-country flying. My wingman's crew kept complaining that their pilot was flying too low, and that they had to keep cleaning pine needles out of the airplane. I told him to raise his altitude and stay out of the pine trees. On his next flight he came in with more pine needles, and he got his final warning just before leaving for a formation flight: If pine needles were found in his plane one more time, he was going to get busted from a flying sergeant to a flying private and made a permanent co-pilot. He was one very angry pilot.

Next, we taxied out as a flight of four, and he was in the number two position. Normally, we took off at thirty-second intervals, using each side of the runway, and circled back to form the formation. I started my takeoff run, but instead of waiting 30 seconds, he started his takeoff at the same time. We lifted off the runway simultaneously. He was so close that his left prop was only three feet from my wing. He nearly took off my right wing. To get away, I kept banking steeper, which did little good, but finally he backed off and assumed his correct position. Later, before any disciplinary action could be taken, he and his crew were all killed in a crash.

One of my crew was from the northeast corner of Tennessee in the Appalachian Mountains area, near the Tri-city airport. On the night of November the 18th, 1942, we took off so he could spend a few hours with his folks. The weather that night was not too good, and it was going to require an instrument approach, using the low-frequency radio range station. (The airport elevation is 1516 MSL. It lies in a valley with 4,000 to 6,000 foot mountains on both sides of the final approach leg.) The initial approach is made down the valley on the east-north-east leg, with the procedure turn on the north side of the range leg. We broke out at about 600 feet, landed on runway 23, and taxied up to a small terminal where the flight service was located.

Seeing the weather getting worse, I asked the crewman to be back in about two hours.

The weather kept getting worse, and the weatherman at the flight service office said that the weather was below minimums, but that he was keeping the airport open so we could leave. Finally, at about 2300 the crewman returned. We loaded up and taxied to the runway 23. By then it was drizzling rain with fog, and the visibility was so low that we could only see two runway lights ahead. We took off, raised the gear, set climb power, and were climbing out in dense raining clouds, on the 245-degree range leg of the radio range. As I looked to the right and said something to the copilot, I saw a house pass just off the right wing. I could see into the lighted living room through a picture window. Immediately, the nose of the aircraft went up, and full power was applied. We didn't stop climbing until we broke out of the clouds at about eleven- thousand. Neither I, nor the people in that house, will ever forget that night, because it must have scared hell out of them. That split second view will always stay with me.

We returned to Columbia Air Base that night, only to learn that my low-flying wingman had crashed near Bowling Green, Kentucky, with a crew of seven, and there were no survivors. They, too, were on a night cross-country and encountering the same weather system. They were about two-hundred miles west and encountered icing that was believed to have caused the crash. That pilot, after almost taking my wing off two days before, had finally run out of experience and altitude at the same time, and he took six good airmen with him. The next day a new B-25 and a new crew were assigned to our squadron, and flight training went on without interruption. In a war, the only important thing is to prepare for combat, and the better trained we were, the more damage we could bring to our enemy, and the better chance we had for survival. There was no time to even think about our losses.

About the first of December, 1942, the 340th Bomb Group transferred its operations to Walterboro, South Carolina, for the final phase of combat training, because it was more isolated. While there, I never once had a day leave or left the air base. We were close to gunnery and bombing ranges at Myrtle Beach. I can still hear the top gunner speaking on the intercom saying: "Tighten her up a little bit, Sir. This is too easy." We were already in a forty-five degree bank, going around the target with both fifty-caliber machine guns firing live ammunition into the target. We could see the tracers going into the target.

On the night of December 13, 1942, we were in the operations office trying to decide where we would go that night, when the operations officer said, "The Chaplain needs a ride to Washington, D.C. Why don't you take him there?" Soon we were off to Washington, D.C., Bolling Field, the military air base that was directly across the river from Washington National Airport. Arriving an hour or two after dark, we were hungry, but we were not allowed to leave the flight line wearing flight suits, and none of us had anything else to wear. We were looking at a wall map, trying to figure out the closest city where we could eat supper, when someone said, "Why don't you jump over to Washington National? They have a very good restaurant in the terminal." There was a runway at Bolling Field, which was aligned with a runway at National, so I asked the tower for a clearance to takeoff from Bolling, jump the river, and land on the runway at National. They quickly refused a clearance, so we took off from Bolling and entered the traffic pattern for National, but a problem developed as our radio failed. It took about thirty minutes to locate a switch that accidentally had been turned off during take-off. The tower at National wasn't too happy with us, as we had really messed up the traffic.

We taxied up to the terminal, and when the seven of us walked into the dining room, we really got a reception that would not soon be forgotten. Everybody wanted to buy dinner for us, and we were seated at a table by the window overlooking the airport and a beautiful view. We finished a wonderful meal for which they would not let us pay, and we never did know whom to thank. As we boarded the B-25 to depart, we could see people standing at the window, watching. Leaving Washington National, we headed west down the old low frequency radio range airway called "Green 5". We passed over Roanoke, and Knoxville, and Chattanooga; then west to Memphis. From Memphis, we flew south to New Orleans, and then east to Jacksonville, and arrived back at Walterboro Air Base around daylight the next morning.

We knew that we were nearing the end of our advance combat training, and that soon we would be leaving for combat. It was my turn to fly home to Little Rock, Arkansas, RON there, and visit my parents. On the morning of December 15, 1942, we filed,

"Walterboro direct to Little Rock". The weather was very good, but there was a cold front that was forecast to arrive in Little Rock later that day after our arrival time. About fifty miles out of Little Rock, we reached the front, which had arrived ahead of the forecast. Having been reared in that country, with several years of flying experience in the area, I decided to follow the railroad tracks into Little Rock and fly under the weather. The rain was so heavy that there was no forward visibility. I not only knew where every water tank was located, but on which side of the railroad tracks the train station was located. The railroad track followed a straight line until it reached an area just outside the city. We lost sight of the railroad track when it made a right turn, as we headed into an area with several tall radio towers.

Climbing into the clouds, calling the tower for an instrument approach clearance, we headed for the low- frequency range station. The tower informed us that the field was closed. I told the tower that we had enough fuel to make only one approach, and that if we had a missed approach, we would have to pull up and bailout. Upon passing the high cone of silence, we turned outbound, letting down to procedure turn altitude, after which we proceeded inbound, descending to low- cone altitude. Having no forward visibility and zero ceiling, I knew that the time and rate of descent to the end of the runway had to be perfect. We hit the runway with only half flaps and a higher than normal speed. It was raining so hard that all we could see were passing runway lights. Applying brakes had no results, so I yelled, "AIR BRAKES". The flight engineer already had his hand on the air brake lever, and he locked the main wheels. There was so much water on the runway that the wheels were hydroplaning, but the B-25 came to a stop with only one- hundred feet of runway left.

For a few minutes we just sat there, trying to pull ourselves together, while the rain poured down. We had "cheated death again". Then the tower called, "Army 616 what is your position?" We answered, "Army 616 has landed, and we are sitting on the end of the runway." The taxiway took us right in front of the tower, and as we passed, we realized it was the first time they had seen us. With air in the hydraulic brake lines, the brakes were jerky and had to be bled to remove all the air.

In less than an hour after we had landed, the rain stopped, and the late afternoon sun came out. The crew went to town, checked into a hotel, and went out on the town. They really enjoyed Little Rock.

My parents and brother were at the airport to meet us, and we had a nice visit. The next morning the crew was at the airport ready to go, but they had picked up an extra airman who was trying to get to Birmingham, Alabama. We had to make a ten-minute hop to Stuttgart, Arkansas, to fuel the plane. Then we were off to Walterboro Air Base. When we reached Birmingham, we encountered the same weather that had closed Little Rock, so we flew on to Walterboro. I took the extra airman to operations office, and they said they would find a way to get him to Birmingham.

About a week before Christmas in 1942, a pilots' meeting was held, and we received a briefing for a flight to the combat zone. For security reasons they briefed us to the Pacific and to the North African theaters. Since the North African invasion had begun on November 8, 1942, we were sure we would be sent to North Africa. We would fly to Miami; Puerto Rico; Georgetown, British Guyana; Belem, Brazil; and to Natal, Brazil. From Natal it was a long hop to the Gold Coast of Africa, with one fuel stop in the middle of the Atlantic Ocean, on one of the Ascension Islands. Following the flight briefing, we were told to report the next morning for a physical exam, and that we could expect to depart Walterboro the following day.

For over a year I had been aware that I had a right inguinal hernia problem, but by tightening my abdominal muscles, I was able to pass a physical exam. However, by that time, it was getting much worse. When the doctor had me turn my head and cough, I could no longer hide the problem. The doctor came unglued and said, "You have been flying in this condition. Don't you realize how dangerous this is? If it had strangulated on you while flying, you would have put the entire crew at risk. You are going straight to the hospital for surgery." In less then an hour, I was being flown in a B-25 to Columbia Army Air Base, and then driven across town in a staff car to the Columbia Army Base Hospital. The shock of leaving my squadron caused me to shed a few tears, but it also saved my life. A couple of years later, I would learn that the original group suffered losses of almost one-hundred-percent by the time they had fought in North Africa, Sicily, and Italy. Without even knowing, I had "cheated death again".

CHAPTER 6
Return to Columbia 1943

The staff car drove up to the officers' ward at the hospital, and I asked the driver to wait, as I wanted him to drop me off at the Wade Hamilton Hotel. Once in the ward, I asked, "How do you get a leave?" One of the patients said, "The ward officer can give you a leave." The only officer around was a first lieutenant nurse, and when she was asked if it were all right to take twenty-four hours to settle some personal matters, she said that it was all right with her. Back into the staff car, I headed to the hotel, as a party looking for a place to happen.

The following afternoon about 1600, things were going so well that it was necessary to call the ward officer and ask for another twenty-four hour leave. A captain answered the phone, and I said, "This is Lieutenant Herrod. I need to extend my leave another twenty-four hours." He interrupted, saying in an angry voice, "Lieutenant Herrod, I am the ward officer, and you are AWOL (Absent With-Out Leave). You are in a lot of trouble, and you better get back here as soon as possible." I said, "Sir, the first lieutenant nurse said it was all right. I thought she was the ward officer." He said, "She is not the ward officer. I am the ward officer." After hurriedly checking out of the hotel, I took a taxi back to the hospital. My orders were to report to the commanding officer of the hospital at 0900 the next morning. Once again, this young cocky second lieutenant was in deep trouble.

At 0900 the next morning, I was standing, at attention, before a full chicken colonel, trying to explain that the first lieutenant nurse had said that it was all right with her, and that I thought she was the ward officer. The look on his face gave me the impression that he was having a hard time not laughing. Without any further conversation, he ordered me to report back to my ward. I ended up being the hospital's biggest joke of the year and immediately became known to all the nurses in the hospital. . Anyone who has been around a hospital during the holidays of Christmas and New Year knows that it's party time, and that any procedures that can be postponed until after the holidays will be postponed. My surgery was postponed until after the holidays. Each night I was invited to a nurse's party, and I would get to bed about 0200 or 0300 every morning, sleep until noon, and then start getting ready for another date. To say that it was a "Merry Christmas and a Happy New Year" is a gross understatement.

After a big New Year party, it was finally time for surgery, and all the nurses provided the best medical advice that any patient ever got. They said that the best surgeon in the hospital was Col. Weaks, and that I should ask for a spinal. On the morning of the surgery an ambulance took me from my ward to the operating room. After the medics put me on the operating table, someone gave me a spinal. Then they blocked my view of the operation, and the only thing I could see was the clock on the wall at the foot of the operating table. It took Doctor Weaks only twenty-three minutes from start to finish, and then everyone left the operating room except one nurse. She was cleaning up the operating room and would come over and wipe the sweat off my face from time to time. I thought she was the most beautiful girl I had ever seen, and when she wiped the sweat off my face, I put my arm around her, and pulled her down for one great kiss. Soon, the ambulance came to transport me back to my ward.

To my surprise, instead of being taken to the twenty-bed sick bay, I was wheeled into a private room, with a private bathroom, located next to the nurse's office. There were two doors into the room, one from the hallway and one from the nurse's office. The ambulance medics left, and in came two nurses with a tall scotch and soda. What a way to recover from surgery! My instructions were to stay in bed for three weeks. However, after experiencing using a bedpan, I would close both doors, get out of bed, and go to my private bathroom. Frankly, I think this speeded the recovery and was the healthy thing to do. Sixty years later this operation is done in an outpatient clinic.

Although there was a hospital lights-out rule at 2200 every night, I would read until midnight with both doors closed,. The night supervising nurse made her rounds at midnight. It became routine: every night at midnight, she would come through the nurse's office and straight into my room. She took enough time to have a cigarette and visit for a few minutes. We both enjoyed this nightly visit.

About a week after the operation I received my promotion to 1st Lieutenant. Being confined to a hospital bed, I found very few ways to get into trouble. However, a big problem arose when we got a new night ward nurse. The first night she was on duty, at ten o'clock she came into my room, reached over, and turned off my reading light saying, "It is ten o'clock, lights out!" I reached up and turned the light back on. She turned it off again. I turned it on, saying, "You will leave this light on." She became angry, and leaving the room, she said, "I am going to report you to the night supervisor." At midnight, the night supervisor walked past her, through the nurse's office, and into my room, closing the door. After that night, the night nurse and I were friendly again, and we never had another problem.

After three weeks, they finally allowed me to get out of bed and get dressed, and soon it was a date every night. When a gentleman went to the nurse's quarters to pick up his date, he would be introduced to all the nurses in the lobby. One night while being introduced to the nurses, I came to a rather unattractive nurse. When she was introduced to me, she said, "Don't you remember me? You kissed me while you were still on the operating table." This shattered my memory of a most beautiful girl in the operating room.

Some doctor must have decided that if this patient were well enough to date all the nurses, he must be well enough to return to active duty. Orders came to report to the Columbia Army Air Base, 309th bombardment group. This was not going to be pleasant duty, serving under the CO who had given me hell after landing a B-25 with the tub down and the guns extended. This was the CO who had ripped my promotion to 1st Lieutenant into small pieces of paper.

After a farewell party and being transported across town to the air base, I reported for duty, more than ready to get my hands on a B-25. I found out that the group had a new commanding officer (CO). What a break! My new duty was to be a B-25 flight instructor, training replacement combat crews. They had stopped forming new combat groups, and they were very busy training crews to replace the losses being suffered in both theaters of war. Instead of going to work flying, I was placed on limited duty and handed orders for a fifteen-day leave. All I wanted to do was to get back in a B-25, but I was off to Little Rock, Arkansas, instead.

Would anyone believe that in just fifteen days, this officer would emerge with a brand new red, 1942 Chevrolet off the show-room floor, and a new wife whom I had known for just ten days? When we returned to Columbia, we rented a furnished house, and I rushed to the air base to start flying, only to be told that I was still on limited duty. Just hanging around operations all day was very boring, so I wrote "Standardization for B-25 Training" and a "Flight Instruction Manual", which I gave to my squadron CO. He took it to the group CO, who accepted it, and ordered it be used for all B-25 training. The group CO sent his thanks for my work, and as a reward, he promised he would give me the first good break that came across his desk. What a deal that turned out to be!

It was March 23, 1942, when the flight sergeant returned me to flight status, and it was wonderful to get back at the controls of a B-25. In the first week back on flight status, I logged over forty hours of flight time. The need for combat replacement crews was critical, and the pressure was on to train as hard and fast as possible. Flight training continued around the clock.

Each flight instructor was given five new students to train. There was always at least one student who was very disappointed because he didn't want to fly bombers; he had his heart set on flying fighters. Not only could I understand and relate to this type of student, but also I had developed a special way to change his mind about flying B-25's. We had a stripped down B-25, and with a half load of gas, it performed like a fighter. With this student in the co-pilot seat, I would do a fast taxi to the runway, a fast checkout, and then a takeoff. Climbing out at a forty-five degree angle was a much higher climb rate than the student had ever experienced before. As soon as we were a safe distance from the air base, I would do a loop, followed by a slow roll, and then dive for the ground, leveling off at treetop height, at a very high speed. We would then pull up to traffic altitude, enter the traffic pattern, and land. After this ride, the student was ready to fly B-25's, and we never heard any more about fighters. It was great to be back in the cockpit of the B-25's checking out pilots, putting together a seven-man crew, and forming a combat team. We were working hard, and I loved every minute of it.

For the first time, my home was not a BOQ; it was a home with a wife. That this was an enjoyable change in lifestyle is an understatement, and little by little my strong desire to fly combat missions started diminishing. Being a B-25 flight instructor, and being home every night, was a great life, and it seemed that this would be my wartime job, but all good things have a way of coming to an end.

Part II

CBI Hump Pilot

CHAPTER 7
Orders

It was the morning of June 11, 1943, in Columbia, South Carolina, around 1100, when the phone rang. A captain at Columbia Air Base headquarters was on the line.

"The colonel promised you the first good assignment that came across his desk as a reward for your work on B-25 Flight Instructor Standardization, and this is the deal he has set up for you: He's offering you orders transferring you to the ATC. If you turn them down, he has agreed to give the orders to me. I'll pay you $1000 to turn them down."

I was exhausted after flying all night as instructor for a B-25 combat replacement crew, and had just crawled into bed at 0600. ATC? A thousand dollars? What's this all about?

"What the hell is the ATC?" I asked, not being able to associate the letters "ATC" with anything military. "It is the Air Transport Command, and the orders read 'domestic cargo' out of Miami, Florida. It's those transport planes you see flying past here every day," the Captain replied.

The message was clear: this was the most ideal wartime, stateside-based assignment any 1st Lieutenant in the Army Air Corps had ever been offered, and the Captain on the other end of the line wanted it! For a moment, thoughts passed through my mind of off-duty hours on the sunny beaches of Florida, and warm evenings in posh Miami hotels with their luxury dining. "I don't know anything about the ATC, but if it is worth a thousand dollars to you, it must be worth a thousand dollars to me. I'll take it."

"OK, but you'll have to get to the base quickly, because you have to catch an Eastern Airlines flight to Miami at 1600. You'll have to check out of the air base before you leave. Get here as quickly as you can, and I'll have a staff car and driver waiting to help you check out."

This sudden turn of events put a temporary hold on two new loves, a new wife and a new 1942 red Chevrolet. Being married three months, and owning a brand new red Chevrolet for two-and-a-half months, had created a change in this young pilot's mind-set. The desire to fly fighters in combat and get the enemy in my gun sites had been replaced with a strong desire to survive the war. Flying domestic cargo out of Miami didn't sound like a bad deal, and we looked forward to getting settled in sunny Florida.

After dropping me at air base headquarters, my wife returned to our apartment to pack my B-4 bag and call her father to come and help her move back home until we could get settled in Miami. She returned to the air base to pick me up. Then she delivered me to the municipal airport just in time to catch an Eastern Airlines DC-3 to Miami. We thought it would be only a week or two before we would be settled in a new home in Miami. Instead, it would be a year-and-a-half before we would see or talk to each other again.

There was one fact that triggered a level of concern in my mind: In addition to my B-4 bag and parachute, the duffel bags that were issued were stuffed with various types of equipment, such as a gas mask, which seemed more appropriate for combat conditions than flying domestic cargo out of Miami. However, this was the Army Air Corps, and things such as this were not to be questioned. A further problem diverted my attention: all those bags caused three passengers to be bumped from the flight to Miami because of the weight.

The flight arrived in Miami at 2100, and my orders were to report to a location in Boca Raton, Florida. After loading my luggage into a cab, I was off for my new assignment. An hour-and-a-half later, on a back road winding through sand dunes, the cab came around a curve into floodlights, and we found ourselves looking down the barrel of a rifle with a fixed bayonet. The sentry ordered the cab to turn around and depart after the luggage was unloaded, and then he made a call on his field phone. Shortly thereafter, a Jeep arrived. The luggage was piled onto the Jeep, and we proceeded through the sand dunes to a nearby army tent. In that "tent of needles", there were a number of men who appeared to be in the same position as I: questioning why we were in this place, and why everyone was receiving injections in various areas of their bodies for every type of disease known to man!

Soon, a closed bus pulled up, and 20 to 30 of us, along with all of our luggage, were taken aboard. We found ourselves on a bus with no windows, being carried to some unknown destination. My previous thoughts of Miami and domestic cargo flying were giving way to thoughts of combat flying in some remote area of the world.

After an hour, the bus stopped, and we stepped into the portal of a beautiful, tropical, luxurious hotel that had been taken over by the military. Rather than being assigned rooms, we were handed secret sealed orders with instructions not to break the seal until

Nearly forty-five minutes later, the bus came to a stop, and we stepped out into the night darkness. We could make out the silhouette of a large four-engine aircraft that was impossible to identify without benefit of light. We stacked our luggage under the left wing, with our parachutes on top of the stack, and waited. Soon, an officer came up, picked up my parachute, and threw it off to one side.

Protesting, I said, "Sir! I am signed out and responsible for that parachute." Even in the dark I could see a silver insignia on his shoulder, and anything silver dictated military courtesy.

He then pointed to my duffel bag and asked, "What is in this duffel bag?" I named everything in the bag, and then he tossed it beside the parachute.

Again I protested, "Sir! They are going to make me pay for all those things." His response was profound: "Son, where you are going, everything is expendable."

The way he accented "everything" insinuated that "expendable" included all of us. I was the first to be relieved of everything except a B4 bag, and soon the rest of the group was given the same treatment. The officer, whoever he was, must have reduced our takeoff weight by 2,000 pounds!

It was painful to think of all the problems that that luggage had caused, including those three "bumped" passengers who were still in Columbia, South Carolina; they were probably still waiting for a flight to Miami! The officer who had had so little regard for our equipment, turned out to be General Alexander, the pilot of our C-82, and the new ATC Commanding General of the CBI Theater.

As we were taking off from Miami, I thought of two things: First, I should forget the domestic cargo dream, including the warm days on the beach in Miami. Second, how would that Captain back in

South Carolina feel now, if he had paid me a thousand dollars for these orders?

Leaving Miami before daylight and heading out over the ocean, I realized that it had been less than twelve hours since I had left my wife back in Columbia. There had been no way to phone her.

Thirty minutes after takeoff, word was sent from the cockpit that we could open our sealed orders. My orders read, "Chabua, Assam, India."

Turning to the officer sitting next to me, I asked, "Where the hell is Assam, India?" He said, "My God! We've caught the Hump!" My next question was, "What's the Hump?"

He explained, "It's a high range of mountains between India and China, and there is a lot of bad weather." My thought at that moment was, "You takeoff, fly instruments, climb, reach cruising altitude, make your instrument approach and land. No problem!" (Just how naïve can a young, arrogant pilot be?) The fact remains that if it had been that simple, we would not have left a trail of wrecked aircraft and dead Americans all over those mountains between India and China!

Between Miami and our first fuel stop in Puerto Rico, someone spotted a submarine lying in clear, shallow Caribbean water, near an unpopulated island. Everyone was excited, and a radio message was sent, reporting the sighting of a German submarine. It had to be an enemy sub, as we had been losing shipping due to enemy subs in the area recently, and no American submarine would have been in those waters. A short time later, we spotted two combat aircraft with depth bombs under their wings, headed toward our reported sighting. Of course, in time of war, there was no way we would hear about the outcome of their mission, but it did create some excitement on board the aircraft.

After a fuel stop in Puerto Rico, we proceeded to Georgetown, British Guyana, where we spent the night. As we approached Georgetown, we could see Devil's Island (the notorious French prison) in the distance, off the shore of French Guyana. Georgetown was located in a dense jungle area, and the sleeping quarters were built up off the ground on high, wooden posts.

The next day we flew to Natal, Brazil, with a fuel stop at Belem, Brazil. As we approached Belem, we crossed the mouth of the Amazon River near the Atlantic Ocean, and the river at this point was about one-hundred miles wide. While we did not leave the airport, we could see the dense jungle that surrounded us. The first two-thirds of the flight from Belem to Natal was over dense jungle standing in shallow water, and not a place we would want to walk out of if we had to bail out.

After a night and a day in Natal, we took off at 2200 and proceeded east for that very long crossing of the Atlantic Ocean. Our destination for this segment of the trip was a very small spot in the ocean called the Ascension Islands. After a quick fuel stop, we were off to the Gold Coast of Africa. After we landed in Africa, and as the aircraft approached the terminal, we could see a crowd of reporters and cameramen awaiting our arrival. Apparently, the world was about to learn that General Alexander, our pilot, was the new ATC Commanding General of the China Burma India Theater of Operations.

In June of 1943, the battle for North Africa forced air traffic to fly across central Africa to Cairo, Egypt. There was only one fuel stop between the Gold Coast and Cairo, and another between Cairo and Karachi, India.

After traveling halfway around the world in five days, we found ourselves at the Karachi Airport Hotel, and the old Army rule of "hurry and wait" was the order of the day.

It had been less than three weeks since the Trident Conference had ended. It was during the last week of May, 1943, at this conference, that Prime Minister Churchill and President Roosevelt finalized the strategy for the defeat of Japan.

Madam Chiang Kai-shek had been a guest at the White House, lobbying to save China from the onslaught of Japanese troops. She was able to convince President Roosevelt to supply our 14th Air Force personnel and the Chinese army troops in the CBI area, by airlifting supplies. Supplies from China were completely cut off, as the Japanese army had closed all seaports and the Burma Road. She had convinced Roosevelt that keeping Japanese troops engaged in that area, and saving China, was in our own best interest. Events had moved so fast that I had beat Madam Chiang Kai-shek back to Asia.

At the airport in Karachi, India, Madam Chiang Kai-shek's C-54 appeared to be having some kind of mechanical trouble. From my room overlooking the terminal ramp, I could see her standing in the open cargo door and pacing around inside the aircraft. It was a very hot day, with the aircraft parked in the sun, and it must have been very uncomfortable. A mechanic working on her C-54 referred to her as "one bitchy woman".

The Karachi airport was a very busy place. There were a lot of new pilots arriving, and a few combat-weary pilots were heading back to the States. There was no problem distinguishing between the new pilots and those returning home. Most of the pilots returning to the states were thin to the point that their eyes were noticeably sunken back into their heads. This was due to the loss of essential body fat. They had batty eye movements, and some had jerky reflexes. My thought at the time was, "If they ever let me get into that condition, going AWOL would be given consideration."

During my stay at the Karachi Airport Hotel, while having lunch with a new doctor friend, I inquired about the condition of those returning pilots. He said, "They are suffering from combat fatigue, dysentery and no telling what else. They have been in this country too long." He went on to say, "If you think they are bad off, I'll take you on my hospital rounds tonight and show you a soldier with China syphilis. It's a type of syphilis that, over hundreds of years, the Chinese have become completely immune to, but we are not." To this day, I have never seen anything as horrible as that night when he exposed that soldier's genitals while changing the dressings. After witnessing that soldier's condition, I realized there would be no problem staying celibate for a year and a half.

Chapter 8
Gaya, India

After staying nearly a month at the Karachi Airport Hotel, waiting for the new airbase to be completed, I was off to a new air base at Gaya, India, for C-46 training. No military personnel had ever occupied the Gaya Air Base; it was populated only by sacred cows and snakes, both of which had to go. Some natives were hired to keep the sacred cows off the base, but we had to take care of the snakes ourselves.

There were only two kinds of snakes that presented a problem: the Cobra and the Krait. Everyone knew what a Cobra looked like, but not the Krait. Both snakes were deadly, but the Krait was one of the most deadly in the world. The Krait was small, only about 12 inches long, and looked like a harmless grass snake, but it certainly changed the way we lived. We slept with mosquito netting carefully tucked under our mattresses to protect us from snakes, rather than the mosquitoes. In the morning great care had to be taken to shake our boots before putting them on our feet, to discover if there had been any nighttime intruders. We were killing ten snakes a day during the first few days, and it took about two weeks to rid our area of the creatures. There were nearly ten pilots in our bamboo basha quarters, and one day we killed a Krait under the bunk of one of the pilots. We were more successful getting rid of the snakes, however, than the natives were with those damned sacred cows; we never did completely rid the base of them.

One evening, shortly after sunset and just before dark, during our first week at Gaya, the native cow patrol guard was walking down the dirt street about twenty feet in front of our bamboo basha. The native was barefoot, dressed with a wrap-around sheet, and a turban on his head. He carried a six-foot pole, which served as a walking stick and weapon. From our position sitting in front of our basha, we saw the native leap straight up and thrust downward with his pole. He had stepped on a cobra, jumped straight up, and killed the snake with his pole, all at the same time. About an hour after witnessing this feat and sharing our favorite snake stories, someone offered a hundred dollars to anyone who would walk barefooted to the latrine, which was only four-hundred feet away. There were no takers.

One evening we heard the beating of native drums in the distance. They sounded like those used by Indians in the old cowboy movies, and they continued day and night. We soon learned that the natives were celebrating the historic massacre of hundreds of British in Calcutta many years earlier.

This area of India was very remote, and we were unsure of the natives' intent and feared the worst. We were ordered to wear sidearms and never be more than three feet from our .45 pistols. The next day rifles and ammunition were issued, all of our native help was dismissed, and a perimeter guard was established. We were never sure they meant us any harm, but our show of force seemed to work. After the holiday remembrance, the drums stopped beating, and everything returned to normal, except that the natives seemed friendlier somehow.

Awakening one morning, I noticed a very large tree trunk standing just outside the door of our basha, where no tree had stood before. Jumping out of bed and running to the door, I discovered a very huge elephant standing just a few feet in front of me. Everyone then proceeded to take elephant rides, and the elephant's keeper did fairly well, selling rides on that enormous animal.

It was customary, when being introduced to a new airplane, to spend many hours in the cockpit getting ready to be checked out on the unfamiliar controls. After logging 2.3 hours as co-pilot, 8.9 hours of dual flight instruction, 8.6 hours as pilot in command and a total of 40 landings, I was off to Chabau to be a Hump pilot. It had been four months since receiving those sealed orders that morning in Miami, and arriving at the assigned destination of Chabua, Assam, India. The old army rule of "hurry and wait" was still in effect.

Chapter 9
Chabua, India Air Base

C-46 Departing Chabua, India

Chabua was in a war zone, and life there was different from what we had been accustomed to at other bases. There were trenches everywhere, to be used as protection from enemy bomb explosions, and everyone was armed. A network of aircraft taxi strips and revetments dispersed all our aircraft. During my first week at Chabua, I had two new traumatic experiences: an air raid and an earthquake!

Chabua Air Base was less than one hour flying time from the nearest Japanese Air Base at Myitkyina, Burma. The Japanese Zero fighters flying out of Myitkyina were used against our unarmed transports, but only during daylight hours, and in good weather. Japanese observation planes kept close watch over our base, however, and each time one flew over, the air raid siren sounded.

The first time we heard an air raid siren, several of us ran to a trench for protection. We were new to Chabua, and at first we were the only ones in the trench, but soon others arrived. Those arriving later carried chairs and something to read. We newcomers stood in that trench for over an hour, waiting for the all-clear signal. All the "old-timers" were sitting in their comfortable chairs, reading something of interest. The next time an air raid siren sounded, we walked to the trench with our chair and reading material and were recognized as experienced "old-timers". We could always tell who was new to the base when the air raid siren sounded, by what comfort materials were taken to the trench.

Basha Mates

There were also a few enemy bomber attacks, but none during my stay at Chabua. However, one time returning from a mission, I had to circle at the north end of the Assam Valley and wait for the Japanese to finish bombing one of our air bases north of Chabua. While we were too far away to see the aircraft, we could see the bombs exploding. The bases at Yunnan and Kunming, China, were different---they did get bombed frequently, and the Chinese had a unique air raid warning system. They had a long pole on which they could raise large paper balls. When one ball was raised, the Japanese planes were airborne. When two balls were raised, the Japanese planes were 20 minutes away. When three balls were raised, the enemy was in sight.

In Kunming, intelligence knew in advance when the Japanese were going to bomb the air base. It was not uncommon to hear someone say, "We are going to get bombed at 1500 this afternoon," or the comment would be, "The bombers are taking off to bomb us." Twenty to thirty minutes before the bombs would start dropping, we would see all aircraft capable of flight departing the airbase. At the same time, non-essential military personnel were heading to the trenches or for the side of a large hill just west of the base. The hillside served as an amphitheater where everyone could sit and watch the bombing.

Basha House Cat

During my first week in Chabua, an earthquake occurred one night about 2100. At first, the bamboo matting that formed the ceiling of our basha started squeaking. Then the bunks started jumping around, and someone yelled; "Earthquake!" The earth was moving so violently that the electric light hanging from the ceiling was swinging in a 90 - degree arc. Everyone ran outside and tried to remain standing as the earth rolled back and forth, and we could hear the sound of dishes crashing in the nearby mess hall. We were all sure that the epicenter was in Japan, the country would be destroyed, the war would be over, and we would be going home soon. The next day we learned that the epicenter was only a couple of miles away and had only destroyed a native village.

It did not take long to start logging combat time. On October 14th, 18th, 20th, and 23rd of 1943, four trips to China were flown, averaging about 6-and-a-half hours each, as copilot in C-46's; three to Kunming, and one to Yunnan. On the 25th of October I made trip number five to Kunming as first pilot. It was the first day of round-the-clock flight operations. Until that time, all Hump flights were conducted during daylight hours. What was to have a 0800 departure

67

turned into a 1900 departure due to mechanical problems, so the newest first pilot in the CBI Theater was on the first night Hump flight.

After being lost during my first two trips over the Hump as pilot-in-command, and ending up south of Kunming in Japanese territory, I knew it was time for me to check out a sextant. With a sextant, a pilot could sit in the cockpit and shoot the North Star through the windshield. Once he determined its angle, it didn't take long for him to calculate his latitude. All he had to do was bracket the latitude of Kunming, and he could not miss his destination. Of course, if he were not on top of all the clouds, the sextant did not help, and he had only weak and jammed signals from the homing stations to help him navigate.

Not once, during my first six trips, had any mountains been seen, due to bad weather. All six trips had been under instrument flight conditions. On the seventh trip, we broke out of the clouds, approaching the Salween River. In full moonlight, two snowcapped ridges were clearly visible out both sides of the airplane. The ridges were running north and south, ninety degrees to our course, and they appeared very close. We were at 17,000 feet, and the maps showed the mountains to be 15,500 feet in height. These mountains were the most beautiful, and at the same time the most fearful sight, a pilot could see. The view made us understand why they called it the "Hump". Those mountains looked a lot closer than 1,500 feet, so we did a little climbing.

Our principle means of navigation was the Automatic Directional Finder (ADF), and we had two units on board. We had a reasonably strong homing station at Chabua; a very weak station at Fort Hertz at the north end of the Hukawng Valley; a weak station at Yunnan, China; and a station in Kunming, China. There are three real problems when using ADF. During thunderstorm activity, the needle will point to thunderstorms, due to the electrical disturbance. It takes lots of experience to tell the difference between the station one is monitoring and the thunderstorms. Another problem can occur when the plane is in icing conditions. When icing conditions prevail, the ADF antenna housing can become covered with ice, causing the ADF not to work. Another annoying problem was that ADF homing stations could be jammed by the Japanese. Part of our route was over Japanese-held territory, and in China, the enemy lines paralleled our route. This made it easy for the Japanese to transmit a stronger signal on the same frequency, causing us to home in on the enemy station, rather than the station we thought we were using.

One night, about 0200, as we were crossing the Hukawng Valley in Burma, heading for Chabua, the enemy was jamming the Fort Hertz station. Their signal was so strong that we were able to plot their location by taking bearings from a known track. Upon landing in Chabua, we reported their location to intelligence, and fighter planes were dispatched that morning at daybreak. The fighters approached the location into the sunrise, and they were able to see the antenna wire because of the sun's reflection, which was caused by the dew collected on the wire. They blasted that station and the Japanese operators out of existence. That stopped the jamming from that area for a while.

ADF was the only available instrument approach until a Low Frequency Range system was installed. With two transmitters aligned with the runway, like the ILS (Instrument Landing System) outer and middle marker of today, and two ADF sets in the aircraft, landing with a 400-foot ceiling and one mile visibility were quite safe. However, there were times when landings were made at or near zero ceiling and visibility.

During the fall and winter months of 1943, losses of planes and crews flying the Hump increased. One out of every seventy-five aircraft that took off didn't make it over the Hump and back. The high loss rate was not attributed to night flying, but more frequently caused by two related factors: enemy action and weather. Actually, the night flights were considered safer than daytime operations! Enemy action in the air was limited to daylight hours and good weather, so passenger flights were limited to night trips only, departing Chabua between 2100 and 2200 each night.

The Japanese enemy airfield at Myitkyina, Burma, was just south of a direct route between Chabua, India, and Kunming, China. Enemy fighter aircraft forced us to fly northern routes, where the mountains were much higher. We were flying at 17,000 feet, and mountaintops on our route were 15,500 feet. Further north of our route, mountain peaks were 18-20,000 feet. Combine this terrain with aircraft at maximum gross weight, inexperienced pilots, enemy aircraft, jet winds at times that were well in excess of 100 miles per hour, icing conditions, thunderstorms, unreliable navigational aids being electronically jammed by the Japanese, and we had very difficult flying conditions.

Today we teach pilots that, "when flying from high to low pressure, they should look out below". For some reason no one gave thought to the fact that anytime we were flying from an area of higher atmospheric pressure to an area of lower atmospheric pressure, we would always be lower than the indicated altitude. The altimeter only senses atmospheric pressure, and will follow a pressure gradient up or down. Normally, a pilot keeps resetting his altimeter to local atmospheric pressure. On a long trip without altimeter settings, there can be a large difference between indicated altitude and true altitude. It's a wonder that our losses were not much greater.

Pilots faced a "Catch 22": If the weather was good, we had Japanese Fighters to contend with. If the weather was bad, we had mountains, icing conditions, turbulence and navigational problems. During the winter of 1943-44, bad weather was preferred to Japanese fighters. One day during that period, the Japanese fighters shot down 14 of our transports.

A pilot friend of mine, named Heller, was returning from China, crossing Burma over the north end of the Hukawng Valley. Looking south through the left cockpit window, all four crewmembers watched two Japanese fighters shooting down a C-46. While watching, they saw bullet holes appear in their own left wing, followed by a Zero pulling up for another pass. Heller dove for a cloudbank, and quickly cranked the rudder trim tab to its stop. This caused the aircraft to skid sideways. The skid caused the Japanese to miss his target. The attacker was pulling up for a third pass, and Heller cranked the rudder trim tab to the opposite stop, causing the aircraft to skid in the opposite direction. The Japanese missed again. Heller then flew into the clouds covering the mountains of the first ridge. Flying in clouds covering mountains tops is dangerous, but it beat letting that Japanese Zero shoot him down. If the Japanese pilot is still alive, he may still be trying to figure out why he couldn't shoot that C-46 down. Then again, by now he may have figured out that in a skid, an aircraft does not fly in the direction it is pointing!

Chapter 10
The Black Market

During my first weeks in Chabua, I learned that money could be made exchanging American currency into 100 Indian Rupee notes. Taking the Rupee notes to China and exchanging them for American currency could make a good profit. A carton of American cigarettes that cost fifty cents in India was worth twenty dollars in China. A fifth of American liquor that cost three dollars in India would bring forty-five to fifty dollars in China. Since there was no other way into or out of China, there must have been many things that would produce such a profit, but was this legal? Nobody I asked really knew for sure.

When the Base Finance Officer was asked if it were legal to exchange money for a profit, he did not know, and suggested that I ask the Wing Finance Officer. When the Wing Finance Officer was asked, he didn't know, and suggested asking the Theater Finance Officer. After a flight to Calcutta from Chabua, there was time to go to CBI headquarters and ask the top Finance Officer. He was a full chicken Colonel. With correct military courtesy and standing at attention, I asked, "Sir, is exchanging money in China legal?" His answer came quickly: "Captain, it is not illegal, but we frown on it." With a "Thank you, Sir!" and a snappy salute, nothing more was said. It was back to the airport for the return flight to Chabua in Assam, India, and into the money-changing business.

Between the weather and Japanese fighter aircraft, odds were 75 to 1 of not making it over the Hump and back. This fact caused me to set a limit of $5,000.00 on the venture. With cash in hand, after borrowing from Captain Cooper, who had the bunk next to me, all was ready.

It is interesting to remember that when one pilot borrowed money from another, he wrote a check on his home bank for the amount due him. The check was put into the borrower's footlocker, which was at the foot of his bunk, and always left unlocked. It was not unusual for a bunk to become empty, if he didn't make it back. Without notification, someone would just come in and take the footlocker away. There was no service or discussion about it: he had just taken a trip, and he wasn't coming back. The checks covering the loan were always good, and there was never anything stolen from an unlocked footlocker.

What was the money-changing business like? In India, one had to have cash in U.S. bills, exchange them for 100 Rupee notes, and then get them to downtown Kunming, China. Once in Kunming, there was no problem getting from the airport to the downtown area for an excellent American dinner. After dinner, one would take a short walk down a dark downtown street. A Chinese, dressed like a coolie, would approach the money carrier as he walked down a street. "Change money?" he would ask. "How much?" was always the reply, and this would start the negotiations.

Once a price was agreed upon, the Chinaman asked, "How you want it, in hundreds or twenties?" Stepping off the street and being led down a dark alley to his place of business, where the exchange was to be made, was a frightening, uncomfortable experience, even though I was armed with a .45 pistol. While it was quasi-legal for us to change money, the Chinese moneychanger would be shot on the spot by the Chinese military, if caught. Twelve dollars was made on every 100 Rupee note, and there were three 100 Rupee notes for each one-hundred dollars. Although a $1,800.00 profit was made on a $5,000.00 exchange, it was not worth the risk.

Taking on a partner solved this problem. A civilian tech representative for Pratt and Whitney Engine Company handled the China side of each transaction for half the profit. Our not having to go into downtown Kunming simplified everything. The exchange was made in his room, which was a short distance from the flight operations office. After returning from China, one needed a day to check all the money, to make sure there were no counterfeit American bills. Surprisingly, no counterfeit money was ever found. Then another exchange into 100 Rupee notes would be made, followed by a quick trip to the flight line to get another trip to China. This routine worked for a short time until a notice appeared on the bulletin board, declaring the changing of money in China to be illegal, and the possession of U.S. dollars was no longer allowed. That ended the money-exchange business for this pilot.

A few weeks after the notice appeared, we started getting a large number of replacements. Co-mingled with the replacements was the army's equivalent of FBI agents. One night at midnight, without any prior warning, all aircraft were stopped at the runway before takeoff. A team of these agents searched each plane. This search lasted until noon the next day before other crews were made aware of it. They charged a large number of crewmembers with smuggling in China. The court-martial trial, for those charged, was an assembly-line affair. The accused stood in front of the court, where the charge was read, and they were asked, "Guilty or not guilty?" All pleaded guilty and were fined $5,000.00, regardless of how great their involvement.

Captain Cooper was caught that night. He pleaded guilty, was fined $5,000.00, and made an agreement to have $25.00 per month deducted from his paycheck. After pleading guilty to the charge, he said, "It will take a long time to pay the fine, and I'll not be getting a promotion any time soon, but the rank of captain isn't bad." After returning from the court proceeding, he opened his footlocker and pulled out $14,000.00 in cash. He took it to the post office and told them to send it to his wife in Tennessee. The surprised soldier said, "Captain, you are not supposed to have any American money, and you will have to fill out a report." Captain Cooper wrote diagonally across the form, "Smuggling in China", and signed the form.

For a long time, everybody felt sorry for Captain Cooper. He had been flying the Hump longer than any other pilot in our group. Nobody could figure out why he had not been rotated back to the states, but the reason for his extended Hump tour soon became clear. He had turned his Hump-flying trips into a real financial success. In retrospect, many of his stories explained his activities.

During an advance by the Japanese army into China, one of our advance air bases had been overrun and captured. Captain Cooper was the pilot of the last plane to take off from that base, and he described seeing the runway and everything else blown up after his plane was in the air. He described being in town prior to that last flight and seeing the Japanese soldiers in civilian dress. They had been sent in ahead of the army to prevent the town from being destroyed. The Chinese army had disappeared, and the Chinese civilians had evacuated in front of the advancing Japanese troops. The gold, diamonds, sapphires and jade he removed from his foot locker might have come from rich Chinese paying to be flown out of that city. It was after he auctioned the jewels, that Captain Cooper received orders sending him home. Before he left Chabua, he told me that his wife had already bought six homes in Tennessee.

Chapter 11
Passenger Flights

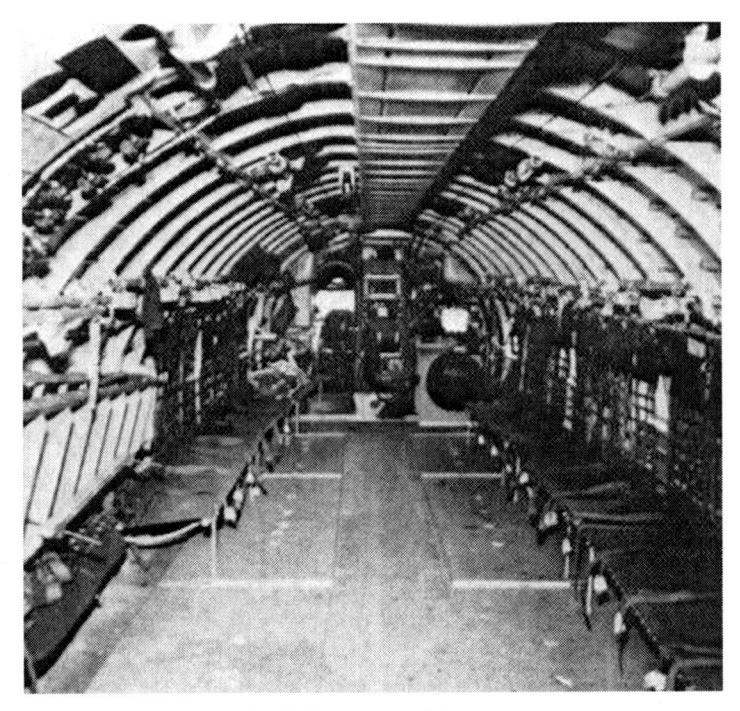

C-46 Passenger Plane

All passengers going to China had to leave from Chabua and take the passenger plane that departed at about 2100 each night. It was equipped with parachutes, oxygen and bucket seats along both sides, between which luggage was secured to the floor. Each flight carried thirty-six passengers and a crew of four. After a weather briefing and necessary paper work, the pilot and copilot would be taken from flight operations to the aircraft revetment. There would be thirty-six scared people waiting at the revetment to board the plane. The pilot and copilot would be the first to climb the ladder to board the aircraft, followed by the passengers. When everyone was seated in bucket seats on each side of the aircraft, the pilot would start the passenger briefing and teach them emergency procedures.

The history of carrying out emergency passenger bailouts was not good. On two separate passenger flights, engine failure required a bailout. In each case, passengers would freeze at the door and refuse to jump. On one flight, the crew was lost because they could not get a passenger to jump, and on another flight, all passengers jumped except one. The crew forced him to the open door. He stood there, pulled his ripcord, popping his chute inside the airplane, and then jumped. The parachute shroud lines were inside by the door; the canopy was inside the fuselage; and the passenger was dangling outside. The crew took a crash ax and cut the shroud lines, releasing the dangling passenger. The pilots then jumped together. It was with this knowledge and a desire to live, that my passenger briefing and procedures were developed.

A loaded C-46 Passenger Plane Departing Chabua, Assam, India

As the passengers came on board, we looked for the biggest, toughest airman, and assigned him a seat by the door. He was shown how to open the door, and given orders to follow, in the event we had to bail out. It was his duty to stand by the door and kick anyone out, even if the passenger hesitated at the door, and that airman was to be the last passenger to bail out.

The passenger briefing started with how to put on, adjust, and use a parachute. Next, it was made clear that in the event we lost an engine over the Hump, there was no way to maintain altitude above the mountain tops, and it would be necessary to bail out. It was also made known that it might be necessary to lighten the load and throw everything located in the center of the cabin overboard. If lightening the load were required, the flight engineer would open the door and supervise the procedure. The passengers were informed that at our cruising altitude of 17,000 feet, the use of oxygen would be necessary, and they were instructed to watch the flight engineer for the signal to put on their oxygen mask and to breathe normally. They were informed of the bailout procedures as follows: They would hear a bell ring. The ringing would alternate on and off. That would be the signal to prepare for bailout. They were to stand up and face the rear of the aircraft. The airman sitting by the door would open the door. Next, the bell would ring steadily. That would be the signal to bailout. Passengers on the left side of the aircraft would then file out first, followed by passengers on the right side. When approaching the door, they should not hesitate! If they hesitated, the airman at the door had orders to kick them out. The bell would ring for one minute, sixty seconds by the clock, after which we, the crew, would leave the cockpit. When we opened the cockpit door, all of them should be gone. If we saw anyone in the aircraft, we would use our cockpit exit to bailout. The passenger would then be in the aircraft by himself.

The truth was that if anyone jumped through the cockpit door, he would be jumping into the prop and wing, but the passengers did not know that. Our purpose was to make the passengers more afraid of not jumping than they were of jumping. We'll never know how effective my briefing was, as no one ever had to bailout of any of my flights.

One night, our crew arrived at the revetment to board the aircraft, only to find all the passengers were Chinese soldiers. The briefing started with a question, "Can anyone translate English to Chinese?" A Chinese soldier volunteered, and the briefing was completed without a problem. After landing in Kunming, we proceeded to the operations office, where the passenger manifest was given to the operations officer. He said, "Captain, you sure had some high rank on board tonight. The lowest ranking officer you had on board was a Brigadier General." We had not been taught to identify Chinese officers' ranks, nor had anyone bothered to read the passenger manifest. Later, we learned that they were Commanding Generals of the Chinese Army, returning from the Cairo Summit conference. The Cairo Summit was held November 23rd through the 26th of 1943, and it affected the lives of all military personnel in the CBI Theater. President Roosevelt, Prime Minster Churchill and Madam Chiang Kai-shek, with their military staffs, set into motion a plan to drive the Japanese out of Northern Burma and capture the airstrip at Myitkyina, Burma.

One night, in Kunming, as we taxied behind the Jeep with the big "follow me" sign to the parking area, there appeared to be a large black circle in the middle of the airfield. The black circle turned out to be hundreds of Chinese soldiers. In the operations office, we were handed a manifest for thirty-six Chinese soldiers to be delivered to Ledo, an airport at the head of the Ledo Road (northeastern Assam, India near the Burma border). Every aircraft leaving Kunming for India that night had Chinese soldiers bound for the same destination. That was the beginning of a military effort to retake Burma; capture the Japanese airfield at Myitkyina, Burma; and reopen the Burma Road. American soldiers were building the Ledo Road that would join the old Burma Road, to open a new land supply route to China. Once inside the lighted airplane cabin, we saw a sad excuse for soldiers. They looked like civilians who had just been herded in from the country. Thank goodness they had no weapons. We did not feel too comfortable, even though both pilots had side-arms.

The passenger briefing proved impossible. No one understood English, and there was no interpreter. We were afraid one of them would open a parachute inside the aircraft, so all passenger parachutes were stored in the rear of the aircraft. After turning off the passenger oxygen, we locked the cockpit door, started the engines, taxied out, took off and started climbing. Our cruising altitude for the trip would be 19,000 feet, where no passenger without oxygen could remain conscious.

That same night, all cargo aircraft carried 36 Chinese soldiers without oxygen or parachutes. Carrying people over the Hump without oxygen or parachutes placed the crew in a position where they could not bailout if an engine were lost. This procedure placed us all in a difficult position and angered many pilots. The problem was solved when all the pilots were assembled in a large, bamboo meeting hall, and a colonel from wing headquarters said, "Here are your orders. If there is a need to abandon the aircraft, you are hereby ordered to leave your passengers in the aircraft and bail out." While some pilots still had questions, I requisitioned a Tommy gun just in case some passenger objected to the pilots leaving the aircraft. Anyway, that was how the Chinese army was airlifted to Burma.

Chapter 12
The Weather Pilots

The powers to be in Washington, D. C., assessed the very high losses of aircraft and crews flying the Hump and came up with two solutions: One, a ground force would be sent into Burma to capture the Japanese airstrip at Myitkyina and re-open the Burma Road; and two, a weather observation system would be established to determine when conditions over the Hump would result in excessive losses. At the time of that decision, there was no way for me to know that I would play a part in both solutions.

Weather Flight Pilot and Co-Pilot

Shortly after being promoted to Captain, orders came for several of us to report to headquarters. When we arrived, we found that there were 16 of us at the meeting. We were told that we were the 16 most experienced pilots below field grade at Chabua, and we were going to fly weather flights. The route between Chabua and Kunming would be divided into 5 segments, and a weather report would be made for each segment. One of us would takeoff every 4 hours, (at 0400, 0800, 1200, 1600, 2000 and 2400), regardless of weather conditions. One of us would also serve at a desk at air traffic control for an 8-hour shift. The pilot on desk duty at Air Traffic Control would be responsible for collecting and analyzing the weather reports, and for determining if the Hump would be open or closed. His order to open or close the Hump could not be rescinded by anyone except the Wing Commanding General. When an aircraft declared an emergency, the pilot on desk duty would take charge of overseeing the plotting of radio directional finding bearings. He was also responsible for a complete report being given to search and rescue.

Weather Pilots with C-46

Flying the Hump, regardless of weather conditions, was a very dangerous undertaking, but little thought was given to this aspect of the job. We did not know that three of us would be killed in weather related crashes during the next two to three months. Militarily, we were trained to carry out an order without question or hesitation. An order is an order. During training before WWII, military law was taught in its entirety. People today do not realize that when their country declares a state of war, constitutional law is modified, and the Articles of War take effect. The Articles of War are now referred to as the "Emergency War Powers Act".

The bright side of this assignment was that we were given a permanent co-pilot, and with only 16 pilots and a flight every 4 hours, we could make the required number of combat trips quickly and then get out of that hell-hole. What we did not know that day was that the required number of trips to be rotated back home would be increased regularly. Replacement pilots were not arriving on schedule, and that made it necessary to raise the combat time requirement frequently.

Taking one's turn as a weather pilot proved to be much easier than desk duty. When the weather was deteriorating, with heavy icing being reported, pilots would plead with the desk duty officer to close the Hump. The Commanding Officer would be on the phone, stating that he was trying to break the tonnage record, and he wanted to keep the Hump open. This put the desk duty officer in a tough spot. These were the precise conditions that existed on my last day of desk duty as a weather pilot.

For the midnight to 0800 duties on the weather desk, it was necessary to be at the operations office by 2300, which enabled the officer to study current weather conditions and check with air traffic control. That night, the weather officer on duty reported heavy icing, and that flying conditions had been getting worse. Air traffic control said they had a couple of aircraft in trouble, and things didn't look good. To make matters worse, incoming pilots were telling horror stories of their flights, and departing pilots were stalling their departures in the hope that the Hump would be closed. Pilots scheduled to depart were begging and pleading that the Hump be closed.

After analyzing the weather and checking with ATC, I didn't take long to make my decision, and I declared that the Hump was closed. This statement was made prior to the start of my duty hour, and the weather pilot on duty said, "The hell it is! You are not on duty until midnight, and until then the Hump is open. The Commanding

Officer is trying to break a tonnage record, and you had better call him before you close it." Air traffic control personnel were listening to the verbal exchange, and word went out all over India and China that the Hump would be closed at midnight. Although it was forty-five minutes to midnight, no further takeoffs were made that night

Calling the Commanding Officer was difficult. After hearing my full briefing, he said, "Captain, those pilots have to fly instruments". My response was, "Sir, if you check their flight logs, you will find 90% of their time lately is instrument time."

My last statement to my commanding officer was, "Sir, if we continue to fly during the next eight to twelve hours, we will lose from eight to fourteen aircraft and their crews. By closing the Hump for a few hours, we will save these aircraft and crewmen, and they will be here tomorrow to carry more tonnage. The weather pilot on duty was given the responsibility to open or close the Hump, and it is my decision that the Hump should be closed, and as long as I am on duty, it is closed." Fifteen minutes later, my replacement arrived, and I was relieved of duty. However, no one rescinded my order, and the Hump remained closed.

Readers will better understand Hump flying after reading about some of our actual flights. While some flights were normal and routine, many were horrible beyond belief. Sixty-nine years later, the memory of those flights is as clear to me as if they happened only yesterday.

Chapter 13
An Instrument Takeoff

It is one thing to practice instrument takeoffs with another pilot ready to correct any mistakes the pilot might make, or to take-off seeing only two or three runway lights ahead of the plane on a foggy night, or just runway centerline marks during the day. However, only in Assam, India, can a pilot experience a one-hundred-percent instrument takeoff.

It was the midnight weather flight, and the Hump was closed, as the weather was terrible. It was raining so hard that the driver could hardly see to find the revetment where the aircraft flight engineer, radio operator and ground crew waited. While making the walk-around inspection, stopping at the landing gear wheel, it was just the right height on which to rest my arms and head. It was one of the few times I really prayed. Whether the prayer was heard, or it was the moment of meditation, all fear was gone, and a feeling of well-being prevailed as we boarded the aircraft and started the engines.

The cockpit floor of a C-46 is twenty-two feet off the ground. It was raining so hard we could see nothing on the ground with the windows closed, not even lights. With the window open, we could see two flashlights from our guide, who was located in the back of a "follow me" Jeep. It was under these conditions that we were led to the end of the runway. The stripes on the runway were used by airmen on the ground to align the aircraft with the runway, and it must have taken at least thirty minutes to get the aircraft properly aligned. To attain alignment, with the cockpit side window open, the pilot waited for two lights to appear on the ground. One light would start moving back and forth. Unlocking the tail wheel, the pilot moved the aircraft as directed. Once in the new position, he stopped. The tail wheel was locked once again, and he waited. Over and over this procedure was repeated, until we saw two lights crossing each other, signaling that alignment was completed. Once the window was closed, nothing was seen outside the cockpit. All that training paid off as we performed a true instrument takeoff. The rest of the trip must have been uneventful as only that takeoff is fully remembered.

Chapter 14
20,000 Feet Looking Up At Mountains

Most people would think there would be no problems on a flight on one of those very rare nights when the weather was good, but they would be wrong! It was about 0100 as we took off from Kunming, China, and turned west for Chabua, India, and the weather was clear, but dark. In fact, it was the best weather I can remember for any flight I made while in that area. We corrected our heading for a forecast twenty-five-knot south wind. At our cruising altitude of 19,000 feet, letting one of those rare things called a "working autopilot" fly the airplane, we passed Tally Lake just west of Yunnan Yi, China. We were a little north of our course. As usual, the navigational radio station was jammed by the Japanese, making our automatic radio directional equipment useless.

About an hour after passing Tally Lake, around 0300, we noticed some clouds appearing. We were flying at their base and made a couple of small course changes to avoid them. As we passed the clouds, we saw they were looking more and more like snow-capped mountains. I asked the copilot to look at them. He said, "I've been watching the same thing on my side but, there are no mountains on this route that are 19,000 feet or higher." Suddenly, we hit strong clear air turbulence. Until then, the air had been glass smooth, and rough air could only be caused by air flowing over a mountain. Immediately, we increased power and started climbing. Soon there were clouds or mountains on both sides of us. At 20,500 feet, looking up at a mountain peak, we could see a streamer of snow. This was the first time we were sure we were looking at mountains. The only mountains this high were far north of our course. We had to be somewhere over Tibet. There were no maps of this area, but some northern portions of our map had blank areas marked "unexplored".

As soon as we could clear the mountains tops, we turned due south, declared an emergency and asked for a bearing. Air traffic control located our position quickly, with class "A" bearings, which meant that the bearings were very accurate. They advised us to fly a 180-degree heading. With a strong head wind, there was a question as to whether we had enough fuel to make it to Chabua. Normal fuel reserve was only forty-five minutes, flight time. With our position being plotted by ground personnel, we were able to lower our altitude and escape much of the headwind. Before landing, I saw that our fuel gauges were reading empty. After landing, the flight engineer walked out on the wing and opened the fuel tanks for a visual check. He reported that no fuel could be seen in the tank. That was close.

Later, we calculated there had been a 135-knot direct crosswind out of the south, which had caused us to be far off course to the north. During the early 1940's, no one flew at 20,000 feet, and the weather people knew little or nothing about upper winds. Had the outside temperature not been within the icing range, we might not have altered course to avoid what we thought were clouds. Had the Japanese not been jamming our homing stations, we might have realized earlier that we were too far north. Had we not had the rare luxury of an operational automatic pilot, we would have been sitting up flying the aircraft, instead of having our seats laid back and us relaxing. The one conclusion we reached was that, "If we make the mistake of thinking a snow-capped mountain is a cloud; it could ruin our whole night."

Himalayan Mountains

Chapter 15
38 Enemy Aircraft Overhead

It was April 26, 1944, and the 0800 weather flight to Kunming, China, was made on an especially bright and sunny day. We had lunch, enjoyed good coffee and delicious chocolate éclairs, and had an equally nice return trip, or so we thought! During lunch, the decision was made to return via the southern, more direct, route with much lower mountainous terrain, as opposed to the far northern route with very high mountainous terrain.

What turned out to be a very dumb decision seemed reasonable at the time. It had been weeks since the last aircraft had been shot down. There were new fighter aircraft flying out of Assam. The Merrill Marauders were fighting in Burma, and the Myitkyina Japanese airstrip had been bombed. The southern route appeared safe to us, so with 4,000 pounds of tungsten strapped to the floor, we took off for Chabua, India.

All eyes were looking down, trying to see some fighting on the ground, as we approached the south end of the Hukawng Valley. A radio warning giving the location of 38 enemy aircraft interrupted our intense observation. Being at the exact location described in the warning, without even looking up, we took a vertical dive for the jungle floor.

The only way our type of aircraft had a chance against a Japanese Zero Fighter was to get on the jungle floor or down low in the mountains. In level, cruise flight, we could be attacked from any direction, but on the deck, we could cover the bottom side, which is the blind side.

A Zero was faster and could fly circles around a transport aircraft, but the transport could make turns with a much smaller radius. During one mission, a C-47 pilot was given credit for downing an attacking Japanese Zero by making a quick turn to miss a mountain, but the Zero was unable to turn sharply enough, and it hit the mountain.

Few pilots have experienced, or ever will experience, a transition from level cruise flight to a vertical dive at cruise power. Nose-down elevator trim is used to maintain the vertical dive. First, the pilot feels the seat belt keeping them from falling into the instrument panel. Next, he notices the air speed passing 360-miles-per-hour, and he starts to worry about how he is going to get out of the dive. Cutting the power greatly increased the forward pressure on the seat belt. Backpressure on the control column had no effect; the elevator was frozen. The elevator trim tab had to be used to start a recovery from the dive, with only about three-to-four-thousand feet of altitude remaining. With the high G-force, our next concern was structural failure. Would the wings withstand this kind of G-force?

After leveling off and heading north on the jungle floor between two mountain ridges, we heard by radio that our fighters were going to attack the enemy aircraft. Someone suggested that we go back and watch the fighters attack, and this sounded like a great idea to the crew. So, with a 90-degree left climbing turn, we left the safety of the jungle floor. This put us on a heading for Chabua, looking for aircraft all the while, hoping to see an air battle.

While no enemy aircraft were seen, we later learned that 28 of the 38 enemy aircraft were shot down. After landing, our aircraft was inspected for structural damage. We expected to find missing wing rivets, the results of excessive G-force, but the only damage was a broken wheel nacelle door arm.

Chapter 16
Barry Goldwater Logs Combat Time

It was the morning of May 3, 1944. After a 0600 wake-up call and breakfast, my co-pilot and I took the shuttle to the weather office. At the airstrip, the lack of activity, and the quiet, indicated to us that the Hump was closed. We were informed by the weather officer, that the midnight weather flight had iced up over the first ridge and almost hadn't made it back, and that the 0400 weather flight had iced up over the first ridge and crashed. He told us that they had not been able to get a weather balloon past 7,000 feet because of the ice. The weather officer said, "The only thing I can tell you is that it is very bad." My copilot was visibly shaken, and you couldn't blame him; our chances on this upcoming flight did not look good.

Walking from the weather office into the flight operations office, the operations officer said, "Major Goldwater is going to be your copilot this morning." My reply was, "The hell he is; I have my own co-pilot!"

Major Goldwater, who was in the operations office interrupted, "Don't you remember me? I was your Physical Training instructor at Luke Field." Without answering his question, I said, "On the weather flights each pilot has his own co-pilot. This is necessary because hand signals must be used to communicate when using oxygen masks. You should cross the Hump when you can see some mountains, and today you won't see anything. You couldn't have chosen a worse time; the flying conditions are really bad. The midnight weather flight iced up and almost went in. The 0400 weather flight iced up and went in on the first ridge. They can't get a weather balloon past 7,000 feet. We don't have a fifty-fifty chance." By that time, my co-pilot was long gone, and I'm sure he was pleased to know that he was not going on this flight!

Goldwater said, "All over the world, all they talk about is how bad the weather is over the Hump. I've waited for it to get this bad just to make this flight! I had to hop a C-47 flight and fly all night just to get here, and I can learn all your hand signals by the time we take off."

Goldwater was right. By the time we took off, all hand signals were understood. While climbing to 17,000 feet, we encountered only light ice. Over the first ridge, we flew into heavy icing, so the anti-icing equipment, using prop alcohol pumping at maximum, was activated. We could hear very loud crashing sounds in the cabin as hunks of ice were being thrown from the props and hitting the fuselage. Those unsettling loud bangs could be music to a Hump pilot's ears, but they could scare the hell out of a person unaccustomed to the sound. While Goldwater jumped when large chunks of ice would hit the side of the fuselage, he never once showed fear or concern.

In the vicinity of the Salween River, once again we ran into heavy icing, and once again the prop alcohol was used at the maximum pump setting. By the time we landed in Kunming, China, we had sent weather reports of heavy icing conditions in two of the five sectors, and instrument weather conditions with light icing, in the other three sectors. The prop alcohol tank was nearly empty, and the flight engineer was instructed to top it off. On the Jeep ride to the operations office in Kunming, we decided to delay the return trip for two or three hours and give the weather a chance to improve. We were in no hurry to fly through heavy icing conditions once again.

We told the operations officer of our plan to delay our return trip and let the weather improve. He said, "Why? The weather must have improved; look at the board!" The board listed all inbound flights. There must have been a hundred airplanes in route to China, all listed on that board. If they were to encounter the same weather we had experienced, one would expect to lose at least 10 to 12 of those aircraft. With the apparent weather improvement, there was no reason to delay the return trip, so after a couple of Chinese éclairs and coffee, we returned to the airplane.

After we climbed the ladder and entered the cabin, we were informed by the flight engineer that there was no prop alcohol in China. This was not welcomed news. If we were unable to prevent ice from forming on the propellers, proper airflow would be destroyed, and we would lose thrust. Ice could also create an imbalance, resulting in a dangerous vibration that could cause structural failure. We concluded that, since the weather had improved, we could make it with the remaining prop alcohol.

After leaving Kunming and climbing to cruise altitude, we found icing in China sectors, where there had been no ice before, and there was still heavy icing in the vicinity of the Salween River. At this point, the flight engineer came into the cockpit and said, "Sir, we are out of prop anti-icing alcohol." This caused real concern, as we had not yet crossed that first ridge where heavy icing had been encountered on our inbound flight. Our chances in heavy icing without prop alcohol were not good.

Usually, on this route there was a large break in the clouds over the Hukawng Valley, located in Northern Burma. If we could find a break in the clouds, descend to the valley floor, fly southwest across the flat jungle floor to intercept and follow the Ledo Road through the pass on the first ridge, we could avoid the heavy icing danger. There was also a new airstrip at Shingbwiyang, Burma, on the Ledo Road, and with this in mind, we altered course a few degrees to the south and headed for the center of the Hukawng Valley.

Suddenly, we broke out of the clouds into a large clear hole, and the jungle could be seen thousands of feet below. Our estimated time of arrival over the Hukawng Valley was correct, and a radio bearing off Fort Hertz confirmed our position. After spiraling down, we found a two to three-thousand-foot ceiling and good visibility. Flying southwest, we intercepted the Ledo Road and tried to follow it through the mountains, but low-hanging scud clouds forced us to make a turn back into the valley. This left us with the choice of the airstrip at Shingbwiyang, or climbing back to cruise altitude and taking our chances with heavy icing with no prop alcohol. We chose Shingbwiyang.

The airstrip at Shingbwiyang was very short. It was on a hillside with mountains on three sides, a cliff on the open end and tall jungle on the high end. Once we were on final approach, we were committed to landing. We made three flybys. My comment each time was, "There's no way to get this airplane on that strip." Each time Goldwater said, "You can do it! Just get it slowed down." We backed off to make a long final approach: slow, with power, hanging on the props and full flaps. I cut the power about three plane lengths from the cliff end of the strip. The plane made a three-point touchdown, and the tail wheel must have been within three feet of the cliff. One would not believe how short, steep and muddy that strip was. We needed to use full power to get to the high end of the strip. After parking, I instructed the flight engineer to remove the 4,000 pounds of tungsten cargo and all but two hours of fuel. We then set out to find a place to spend the night.

The much improved and lengthened Shinbuiyang Airstrip
(When Goldwater and I landed on this strip, it all looked like the muddy ruts in the right foreground. This picture was taken standing near the edge of the Ledo Road looking northeast into the Hukayng Valley, which is about 75 miles square, very flat and contains the most dense jungle in the world. Behind the camera, to the right and left are mountains. In the distance you could see more mountains. They were 15,500 feet enroute to China and over 20,000 feet to the north.)

Landing at Shingbwiyang, Burma, provided us with a ground view look at the incredible Burma jungle, something we had only seen from the air. The tops of the trees looked to be two to three-hundred feet above the jungle floor. For the first time, we had an appreciation for what the crewmembers who had bailed out over this kind of territory and made it back, were talking about. First, they had to make a successful parachute jump. Secondly, if they were hanging in their parachute harness in the top of a tree, they had to find a way to get to the ground without injury. After descending through several layers of jungle growth and reaching the ground, they had to make their way through the thick undergrowth by hacking their way with a machete or crawling like a snake. Then they had to find a native trail, stream or elephant trail to follow. Sooner or later, they would either be captured by the Japanese or run into a native of the area who would do one of two things: either help them return or sell them to the Japanese. If the Japanese took someone prisoner, the captive would be faced with torture and death within 48 hours. Add to this the threat of wild animals, snakes and infectious blood-sucking leeches. The Burma jungle was not a desirable place to jump out of an airplane!

Goldwater's desire for adventure was being fulfilled. We were driven down the newly constructed Ledo Road to spend the night in a forward hospital near the fighting.

The big story that night was about Chinese troops who had come into the hospital tent movie theater the previous night and captured a downed Japanese airman. The Japanese had been shot down and somehow had taken a Chinese soldier's uniform, and he was sitting in the hospital theater, watching the movie. The Americans thought he was a Chinese soldier until the Chinese identified him and took him prisoner. The Americans wanted to interrogate the Japanese airman, as he had been with a flight of 38 enemy bombers and fighters attacking us three days earlier. Our fighters had shot down 28 of the 38 Japanese aircraft that day. The Americans tried to take the Japanese from the Chinese for interrogation, and followed their truck down the road, but the Chinese soldiers solved the problem quickly. They stopped in the middle of the road, took the Japanese out and shot him, and then got back in their truck and left.

The next morning, as we arrived at the landing strip, the sun was shining, and things were much drier. With the cargo and all excess fuel removed, the gross weight of the aircraft was lower than the day before. We were prepared for the shortest takeoff in the history of a C-46 aircraft. The tail of the aircraft was as far into the jungle as we could get it, with the brakes locked. Sitting in that high cockpit, looking down a 15% grade to the end of the airstrip, was a sight that one would never forget. Slowly increasing the power to maximum, plus a little more for luck, we released the brakes. To our surprise, there was room to spare. That airplane jumped into the air in about five plane lengths.

One-hour and thirty-minutes later, we landed at Chabua, India, and taxied to the revetment. We used Goldwater's 35mm camera to take pictures of each other standing at the right engine propeller of the C-46. At that time we could not get any information out by mail, and since Goldwater returned to the states often, he promised to write my wife and send her a picture. It wasn't long before she received a five-page letter and an 8" by 10" colored photograph. Before parting, Goldwater extended an invitation to come to Karachi, India, to get checked out in a C-54.

It would be twenty years later before the complete picture of how Goldwater happened to be in Chabua, and be assigned, as my co-pilot, would be made clear. The story would unfold after flying Senator Barry Goldwater from Billings, Montana, to Greybull, Wyoming, for a political speech. That night, while we were sharing a fifth of Old Crow and reliving our war days, two facts were made known to me for the first time: First, my Commanding Officer in Chabua, Colonel Baker, and Major Goldwater were very good friends, as they had served together in Wilmington, Delaware. When Colonel Baker was transferred to Chabau, Goldwater was sent to Karachi, India, to serve as CBI (China-Burma-India) liaison officer for Crescent Airlines, which was a military airline flying C-54's and supplying the CBI Theater. This accounted for Goldwater's ability to get assigned as my co-pilot.

Secondly, while I had been stationed at Luke Field in March of 1942, taking advanced flight training, my instructor had caught me doing two slow rolls around my friend's airplane, and he was one very angry instructor. After landing, he had stood on the wing of my parked AT-6, screaming, "You've had it! You'll be a civilian tomorrow." It was my Physical Training instructor, Barry Goldwater, who had argued on my behalf at the hearing that saved my military career.

Chapter 17
Heavy Icing

    For the 0400 weather flight, we were scheduled to arrive at the operations office one hour before flight time. Our first stop was at the weather office, where we received a complete update on the Hump weather conditions. The Hump was closed to all traffic due to icing, and the terminal weather was 200-foot ceiling and visibility at one-quarter mile. There was only one good thing about weather like this: One didn't need to worry about enemy aircraft. The 0400 weather flight take-off and climb were routine. Upon reaching 16,000 feet, we broke out and leveled off at 17,000 feet, our cruising altitude. Daylight was beginning to lighten the sky. There was enough light to see that we were in the clear between cloud layers.

    As we approached the first ridge, we were looking into complete blackness. Anticipating ice, we activated the prop alcohol, and turned to maximum. The aircraft had a red nose light that reflected a reddish glow when in the clouds, and suddenly, in the red glow, we could see ice covering the windshield. I grabbed the hand-held spotlight, to check on how much wing ice there was, and discovered there was ice covering the side cockpit window. Looking out of the aft cockpit window, behind the pilot seat, I saw ice also covering this aft side window. Next, the flight instruments indicated the aircraft was losing altitude. With full power and already in high blower, to produce maximum power, we commenced a 180-degree turn. Declaring an emergency, the radio operator sent a "mayday" distress call. In anticipation of having to bail out, the engineer was sent to open the rear door to prevent it from icing over. We all realized the cargo on this trip was of a size that could not be jettisoned. By the time we had completed the 180-degree turn, the radio operator and flight engineer had put on their parachutes. The radio operator said, "Damn it! This is the third time this month I've been in trouble." Although he was starting to cry and breaking under the emotional stress, he was still transmitting a distress signal and performing his duties.

On the present heading, each time we tried to hold altitude, the airspeed would drop. Just before stalling, the nose was lowered to gain speed, but as a result, we lost more altitude, bringing us closer to the mountaintops. Finally, at 10,000 feet, at full throttle and in high blower, we found that the aircraft would hold level flight without stalling. With all four of us in the cockpit, I explained the situation: "We are one hour out of Chabau, over the Hukawng Valley and Burma's most dense jungle area. The jungle would be almost impossible to penetrate. We are exceeding the maximum horsepower output of the engines, and there is no way to tell how long they will last. If one engine should fail, the aircraft will probably stall and go into a spin, and if that happens, don't wait; jump, if you can. Once the airplane goes into a spin, centrifugal force will pin you to a wall, and you won't be able to get out of the aircraft. We are at 10,000 feet, and must cross the first ridge with mountaintops from 9,000 to 11,500 feet high, and under these conditions we have a good chance of hitting a mountain. We are going to take a vote as to whether to bail out or stay with the airplane." The vote was three to one to stay with the airplane; the three crew members out-voted the pilot in command!

The radio operator's seat was just behind the co-pilot. He could be heard trying to make radio contact, calling, "Mayday, Mayday", and then giving a long count. He started to lose it, crying and babbling something about his mother, but the red transmitter light stayed on, indicating that he was still trying to make radio contact. Hopefully, by some remote chance, the signal was getting out to the many directional finders located in the area, and that they were taking bearings on us and sending them to Chabua where they would be plotted. We all knew that when an aircraft was loaded with ice, there was very little chance of radio transmissions being strong enough to get through. When we reached our estimated time of arrival for Chabua, we made a shallow left turn. We could then conclude that we had missed the mountains, passing the first ridge, and that our location was somewhere over the Assam Valley. We all knew that if we had to bail out then, it would be reasonably safe, and that we were not over enemy territory. But first, we made one last attempt at radio contact.

Picking up the mike, I called the Chabua tower, and received a weak answer. The tower informed us that they had only "C" class bearings. "C" class bearings were very poor, and unreliable, so they asked us to fly a heading of 360 degrees so they could check the bearing. We realized that with all the structural ice, bearings were not likely to improve, and flying north would take us toward the very high mountains. Our reply to Chabua tower was, "We have completed a 360 degree turn and have not yet hit a mountain, and we are not going to leave this turn."

Normally, there would be a hundred aircraft in the air between India and China, and ground operations would cause continuous engine noise. This would prohibit tower personnel from hearing incoming aircraft, but not this morning, because the Hump was closed. We advised the tower that we were going to let the props run away, and we asked them to go outside to see if they could hear us. With full power and in high blower, the prop levers were pushed to the forward stop, which momentarily increased the prop speed to over 3,000 RPM, sending the prop tips to a speed beyond the speed of sound. This made one hell of a roar, and it worked! A minute or so later, the tower operator said, "I heard you! You are just northeast of the field," and with that assurance, we started our descent.

At 7,000 feet the temperature was just above freezing, and the automatic radio directional finding equipment began working again. It wasn't long before the ice flew off the windshield, and we had our first look outside the cockpit. We were between two layers of clouds, and we could see ice on the wings. It was clear ice with a perfectly smooth contour, creating the best possible airfoil. When a section broke off behind the prop in the slipstream, we estimated the thickness to be 18 inches.

With the icing conditions and the mountains behind us, we were still not out of trouble. The radio operator was a complete basket-case, and an ambulance had to be ordered to meet the plane. The tower reported a ceiling of indefinite 200 feet and ¼ mile visibility. After circling for 30 minutes to let the ice melt, we descended into the lower clouds and started our instrument approach. The ADF approach was not bad for its day. We had two ADF's in the airplane, and two ground stations aligned with the runway. This was much like today's outer and middle markers, and a 200-foot ceiling was tolerable. After a nice approach and landing, the aircraft rolled to a stop on the runway.

The flight engineer opened the door and dropped the ladder, as the ambulance drove up to the door. The medics came aboard to lead the radio operator away, but when they found out that no one could fill out the paperwork or even sign his name, all of us were instructed to get in the ambulance. I pulled my rank and refused to go to the hospital, but I had a good reason! It was standing procedure for me to report to the flight surgeon for a physical exam after each trip, and after the exam, he would give me a drink of the best combat booze, which really helped me to sleep.

Chapter 18
Pilot Combat Fatigue

It is difficult to understand combat fatigue. It is not apparent to someone that he has been affected by it, but it can be recognized in other pilots. There is a slight unnatural movement of the eyes, sometimes a twitch. It is often evidenced in speech patterns. They might change the subject in the middle of a sentence, but no one would say anything about it to us, since we were all having the same problem. It must be understood that most of the pilots were suffering from chronic diarrhea and weight loss to the point that they had lost essential fat, leaving their eyes sunken into their heads. A bottle of paregoric, to control the diarrhea, was standard equipment; no one went anywhere without it. When someone new from the States mixed with the group, he stood out like a sore thumb: there was no trouble picking out the newcomer!

After someone had flown his first few trips over the Hump, it was not uncommon for him to sleep for 12 hours straight upon his return. As time wore on, he would begin to sleep less and less. After three months flying the Hump, he would come in from a trip, and sit down and play bridge for eight to twelve hours, to try to relax enough to go to sleep.

A problem would usually show up during a routine physical exam. Part of the physical exam for pilots was called the Schneider Test, which involved measuring one's heart rate at rest and after exercise. During one of my exams, I was made to repeat the test three times, and I began to wonder what was wrong. The doctor said, "No matter what, your heart rate stays at 125. We are taking you to the hospital." During the hospital stay, morphine was used to induce rest and relaxation, and after a week in the hospital, I was off to Calcutta for a week of "rehabilitation".

This was absolutely the worst place to go for R & R. Arriving at Dum Dum Airport in Calcutta, I'll never forget the ride to the Grand Hotel.

It was during the very height of the great famine of 1943. We drove through crowds of people, sacred cows, and oxen pulling carts. It looked as if all but the sacred cows were dead, sick or dying. Having studied insect infestations that caused dying due to overpopulation, I felt it disturbingly easy to think in those terms.

Grand Hotel

The inside of the Grand Hotel was like another world. It was the best of British splendor and elegance. There was the mid-afternoon tea time with British Officers, followed by a cocktail hour or two before dinner. Dinner was served with linen, silver and four or five waiters for each person. As soon as I took a sip of water, my glass would immediately be refilled. There was live music playing, while we dined, and everything was great, as long as we didn't look, or go, outside.

From one side of the hotel, we could look down and see 700 to 1,000 natives gathering, waiting for the hotel garbage to be thrown out. From the other side of the hotel, we could see a park, with a street down the middle, which served as an RAF fighter strip. During that period Japanese air raid alerts were common in Calcutta, and at night the city was completely blacked out. One night, another pilot and I attempted to go outside. After stumbling over dead bodies and being unable to see anything in the dark, we quickly returned to the hotel.

Each morning at daybreak, we would see trucks picking up the dead and stacking them like cordwood being hauled away.

After spending a week in Calcutta, I went back to Chabua. Flying the Hump quickly got worse. Increased Japanese fighter activity forced us to fly further north of our direct route and into the area of higher mountains. Any break in the weather brought out the Japanese Zeroes, and a slow flying transport plane did not have a chance. Pilots were making a round trip every other day, and all the crews were logging combat time very quickly. It didn't take long to reach the required number to be sent back to the States, but the only problem was that they kept increasing the required amount of combat time for rotation, and this had a demoralizing effect on everyone.

Several days after the heavy icing trip, when the entire crew was taken to the hospital, the psychological effects caught up with me. It is hard now to visualize how I came to, and found myself on a jungle road. I didn't know where I was or how I got there, or how long I had been there. As I stood there, an army 6 X 6 truck came down the road. I stepped into the middle of the road, flagged it to a stop, climbed into the cab, and said, "Take me straight to the Base Hospital."

That was my second trip to the hospital. The treatment was the same: I was given morphine and a couple of days' rest under observation. This was followed by a seven-day R & R (Rest and Relaxation leave) with two days in Agra, India, and six days in Bombay.

In Agra, we visited the Taj Mahal and climbed one of the four towers. There was also an old medieval fort, complete with an entrance for the elephants. Four of us ended up in the same compartment on the all-night train ride to Bombay, and some of the guys made the mistake of taking along a bottle of Indian rotgut gin. Waking up in a ceiling luggage rack the next morning was horrible. With a very dry mouth, a headache and a sick feeling in the stomach, I remembered the can of tomato juice in my B-4 bag. Before it was possible for me to take a drink, the other three awoke, asking for a drink. When the juice container made it back to me, it was empty. It was the most disappointing moment of my life.

Bombay, India, was a huge port city with strange people, strange language, strange customs, and a strange smell. Checking into the beautiful, luxurious Taj Mahal Hotel placed us in a different world. Later that day, while passing the desk, I heard the clerk tell a Major that there were no vacancies. I said, "Major, I have two beds in my room, and you are welcome to share the room with me," and this meeting turned out to be the most interesting part of the whole trip.

The Major was an army officer, and we ended the day having dinner together. He treated me as if he thought I was an enemy spy, which I believe he thought I was. Although the conversation covered all my duties, he did not explain what an infantry officer was doing in Bombay, India. We would have breakfast and dinner together, but during the day he was drawing supplies and equipment. He finally reached the conclusion that he was not living with an enemy spy, and what a story he had to tell.

He told the horror stories of a year of jungle fighting at Guadalcanal in the South Pacific Theater. Surviving in this hot, wet, muddy and steaming jungle was challenge enough, but added to this were the savage fighting and disease-carrying insects. He described finding American soldiers that the Japanese had cannibalized, and all of those experiences had produced a person whose hatred for the Japanese was unbelievable. Just talking about them caused his face to become red, and I could see his muscles become tense. By his own admission, his only objective in life was to kill Japanese, and he told me there were 3,000 more just like him, who had arrived in Bombay from the South Pacific on the ship, "USS Lurline".

After fighting the Japanese for a year, they had volunteered for a special mission. Later, they became known as the famous Merrill's' Marauders. After the 3,000 Marauders fought their way through northern Burma, destroying three Japanese divisions and taking only three prisoners, there were only about 600 Marauders left because the Japanese took no prisoners. Of those who survived these battles, 100% were mental casualties, and 95% were physical casualties. Having been a pilot, flying behind Jap lines, and landing under fire to evacuate the wounded Marauders to the Ledo, India, hospital, I can say that pilot combat fatigue was nothing when compared to what the Marauders suffered. Little do people realize, or appreciate, the prolonged suffering those men endured.

The Major told one comical story. While fighting in the South Pacific, he had a soldier in his outfit from the mountains of Tennessee. This person was illiterate and undisciplined, and he could not conform to military life, but he was very much at home in the jungle. Until he was drafted, he had never been out of the woods. Every few days he would take off by himself and go hunting. Later, as they advanced, they would find a few dead Japanese soldiers. One day this soldier saw that our artillery was being aimed at a particular hill, and he said to the major, "Ain't any use to shoot at that there hill. Ain't nothing up there but two dead Japs and a sick one," but the battle plan was carried out. After the artillery barrage and attacking the hill, they found just three dead Japanese.

As my room-mate and I parted in Bombay, he said, "We may meet again". While we never did meet again, it was only a few weeks later that I was flying a hospital ship, with a doctor and medics aboard, landing under fire deep in Japanese territory, and evacuating wounded Marauders.

Returning to Chabua after R & R, I was back in the same routine. General Harden, our wing commander, had stopped long enough to make his famous statement, "Under my command there is no such thing as pilot fatigue". He ordered all pilots who had been grounded for combat fatigue, returned to flight status. In reality, he had little choice. We had gone through the winter without replacement, and grounding pilots for medical reasons placed an unacceptable workload on those of us deemed well enough to fly. For months we were making a round trip every other day. It was a reminder of what General Alexander had said long ago at the airport in Miami, "Son, where you are going, everything is expendable."

How bad did it get? One morning five of us were ordered to meet at headquarters at 1500. It was in the spring of 1944, and new pilot replacements were starting to arrive. A fresh new pilot was assigned the job of establishing a training system for checking out the new pilot replacements. The five of us, who were the most experienced, were picked to carry out his training plan. As the officer in charge was explaining the plan, one pilot in the group of five kept saying, "It won't work. I know it won't work, and I don't want any part of it." Each time he made the statement, the officer in charge said, "I understand, Captain, and you are excused", but the pilot just sat there staring ahead.

This pilot was one of the many grounded pilots put back on flight status before he had completely recovered, and it was obvious that he didn't know where he was or what was going on. That very night, at about 2200 during a rainy instrument takeoff, his plane went down a couple miles off the end of the runway. Not only were the four-crew members killed, but also a few hundred Indian natives. The aircraft crashed, perfectly aligned on a road with native huts on either side. The aircraft had 1,000 gallons of 100-octane aviation gas, an 8,000-pound cargo of mortar shells, and barrels of prop alcohol. If the fire hadn't killed them, then the exploding mortar shells did.

As pressure increased to get more and more supplies to China, we were making more round trips over the Hump. After returning from each trip, I went straight to the flight surgeon. My flight surgeon at this time was Dr. John Smith, from Little Rock, Arkansas; that gave us something in common. A close friendship formed that lasted until his death in the mid-1970's. During that time he had an unlimited supply of 180-proof grain medicinal alcohol, and I had an unlimited supply of canned grapefruit juice. I couldn't stand to drink either of those liquids without the other, but together they could be tolerated.

One day, during a routine physical exam, after a round trip to China, the doctor's phone rang. There was an emergency at the flight line. A shot-up B-24 bomber with two engines out was coming in for a crash landing. I had just made an instrument approach with a 400-foot ceiling and very low visibility due to rain and fog, and it was clear that this crew was going to have a real problem.

Doctor John, a nurse, and I jumped into a Jeep and headed for the flight line. Just as we turned onto the road to the flight line, we saw the B-24 pass overhead, flying low with the bomb-bay doors open. The arms and legs of a crewman could be seen, as he jumped from the aircraft. We saw him drop behind the trees, and we could see the parachute start to come out of the pack, but we could not see it open. Doctor John was driving and trying to watch the B-24 at the same time, when suddenly, the nurse screamed. We had almost run over an airman lying in the middle of the road, his parachute lying around him. The nurse and I jumped out of the Jeep to care for the airman in the road, and John drove to take care of the airman we had seen go behind the trees. We all figured he was a goner.

The nurse and I took the airman back to the medical dispensary, and soon all the nine crewmembers began arriving, none with any major injuries. It was unbelievable. Even the airman who had gone down behind the trees without an open parachute was uninjured. He said, "I felt a jerk, and my feet were on the ground." After all the crewmembers had bailed out, at an altitude of 300 to 400 feet, the crippled aircraft crashed and burned off the end of the runway.

One airman told the story of landing just outside an open window of the parachute building. A soldier inside was standing at a table, packing a parachute. He came outside, gathered the parachute over his arm, and waited as the airman unbuckled, so he could take it back into the building for re-packing. The only thing he said was, "I'll take care of your chute." The crewman had to follow him into the building to get directions for the way back to the base. This time he said nothing, but just pointed down the jungle road. It was as if someone were landing by that window every ten minutes. We all had a good laugh over that one!

On another day, during a physical exam following a trip, John said, "I've got orders back to the States, and I can send you back on a medical before I leave." American Airlines had made a commitment to hire me as soon as a separation from the Army Air Corps was signed. With a medical on my record, an airline pilot job was unlikely. Besides, three more round trips to China would give me the required combat time for rotation back to the States, so I declined the opportunity. John understood, and returned to the States. After his departure, the required combat time was increased, and my Hump flying continued.

On an average for every 75 trips over the Hump, two pilots and two airmen were lost, and making a trip every other day reduced one's chances of survival. Someone might ask, "How do men cope with high losses month after month?" As a 22-year-old pilot, with the rank of Captain in the U. S. Army Air Corps, I believed that there were four factors to the answer.

First, one had no choice! We had taken an oath to defend our country and uphold its' Constitution. Anyone without the moral fiber and character to carry out his duty and obey orders would not have been accepted in the first place. In addition to this personal responsibility, there was the physical and mental training, which conditioned everyone to cope with the situation.

Second, was the youth factor! The mindset of a young man makes him invincible. My own thoughts at the time were that I was much better trained, more skilled, and had much more experience than those who were dying. One can call it arrogance, over-confidence, or stupidity, but this attitude has an effect on how losses are accepted.

The third factor is the association with other pilots. We avoided getting to know anyone too well. We could play bridge for hours, and the conversation would be limited to bidding our hands. The only pilot's name I can remember is Captain Cooper, not because he slept in the next bunk, but because he was involved in changing money in the black market. I never did know his first name. Not becoming too familiar with other pilots helped us cope with a pilot's death.

The fourth factor was the way losses were handled. When a pilot was killed, someone would come and pick up his footlocker at the end of his bunk. They would also remove the bedding and collect any personal belongings. That was it; nothing else was said or done. He had just taken a trip and was not coming back. Soon, another pilot would be assigned to that empty bunk.

Chapter 19
Battle for Imphal Valley

In the spring of 1944, we all knew the fighting in northern Burma was getting heavy. The Japanese were attacking the British in the Imphal Valley, just to the southwest of Chabua Air Base. No one was greatly concerned because Lord Louis Mountbatten, the supreme CBI Allied Commander, had met with the pilots in Chabua and assured everyone that the British had everything under control. He said, "The Japanese cannot bring artillery or tanks through the jungle mountains. The British artillery and tanks can take care of the Japanese, and we will not need any help from the Americans." It was this assurance that led us to overlook the fact that a short distance away, all British women and children were being loaded onto aircraft and evacuated from Assam, India.

The Japanese didn't need to bring their artillery and tanks. They had captured some of the British artillery and tanks and used them to their advantage, which changed the tide of the battle. It was not long before the British were calling for help from the Americans. Transport planes were diverted from Hump flying and used to carry troops and supplies into battle.

About this time several of us were told to report to headquarters, where we were given some very disturbing news. The officer in charge said, "Intelligence has lost track of one of three Japanese Imperial Army divisions attacking the British in the Imphal Valley. Intelligence believes this Japanese division will try to cut the railroad supply line and attack our air bases. We are not ready to release this information, so keep it to ourselves. Each of you will be assigned an area of the air base to secure. Rifles and ammunition are being issued. Native work details are clearing the jungle to provide a protective area."

Any one of us could have sat behind a gun sight in a fighter plane and won an air battle, but on the ground, we didn't know one end of a rifle from the other. We all had received a few hours on the rifle range, but ground fighting had not been part of our training. This fact became a minor detail, as my assignment was to secure the mechanics' living area of the air base.

By nightfall, the native detail clearing the jungle was able to clear a 30-foot-wide perimeter for the guards to patrol, and at 1800 a guard detail of about 30 men assembled outside the office for the Officer of the Day. All were mechanics who had just returned from 8 to 12 hours of hard work. They were very unhappy about doing guard duty.

As the Sergeant of the Guard ordered, "Left Face", one by one, the men turned left. As the order, "Forward March", was given, they started walking away. It was very clear that, for the safety of all, the reason and need for guard duty had to be explained. I ordered the Sergeant of the Guard to return his men, after they had walked a few steps.

Being in charge of this group, I made the decision to explain the situation, which included the dangers they were facing, and the importance of their duty to protect the area. When they realized the facts and the seriousness of our situation, they were transformed from tired mechanics into very disciplined soldiers. Then, when the Sergeant of the Guard said, "Attention!" they snapped to like West Point cadets. When the command, "Left Face", was given, it was executed with military precision, and with "Forward March", they marched away as soldiers. As airmen, they may not have known much about the rifles they were carrying, but I was sure they could be depended upon to guard the area that night.

Around 2100 that same evening, a Jeep drove up to the Officer of the Day office, and the Staff Sergeant driver said, "Captain, you had better do something about those guards at the gate before they kill someone." He told me that as his vehicle had approached the gate, the guard had come at them with his rifle and bayonet. "He made us get out of the Jeep, come forward in the headlights, lay our identification on the ground, and back off while it was inspected. The guards didn't even have the safety locks on their rifles." The Sergeant of the Guard was advised to make sure in the future his men had their rifle safety locks on.

Later, about 0230, a rifle fired, and I jumped up and ran out of the office toward the gate with my .45 drawn. After running a few feet, I came to a stop, turned and walked back to the office, realizing the stupidity of my actions, and how quickly one's own guard could shoot me. Shortly thereafter, the Sergeant of the Guard came to the office to report that one of the airmen had stumbled and accidentally discharged his rifle. They were working in pairs, back to back, and everyone had his rifle safety lock off. It's a wonder we didn't kill one of our own people that night. The danger was real, as we later learned that the Japanese had blocked the railroad for a short time, just 15 miles southwest of our base.

Later that morning, another officer arrived to relieve me, with orders for me to report to headquarters. There were only three pilots on the airbase with B-25 experience, and we were being ordered to catch a ride on a passenger plane to an airbase near Calcutta. We were to pick-up B-25's that would haul ammunition into the Imphal Valley. The bomb-bays of those medium twin-engine bombers were going to be used to carry ammunition to the British, who were reported to be losing the battle with the Japanese in that area. Carrying ammunition into a battle zone that was under fire did not sound like a safe operation to me, but we hitched a ride to pick up the planes as ordered.

We deplaned at an airbase somewhere northeast of Calcutta and walked to the operations office. The Operations Officer said, "I need one of you to pick up a B-25 in Karachi." I quickly accepted the assignment and re-boarded the passenger plane. Being sent to Karachi would give me the opportunity to see Major Goldwater and to get checked out in a C-54, as he had promised the month before.

The C-54 was the largest transport plane the Army Air Corps had at the time. It had four engines and a tricycle landing gear, and it looked huge when compared to other aircraft.

After getting off the airplane in Karachi, I went straight to Goldwater's Crescent Airlines office and announced my readiness for a C-54 checkout. Goldwater said, "I'm not only going to check you out on a C-54, but we are going to Cairo, Egypt, for a party." My response was, "O.K., but first I have to report to the Operations Officer".

Upon reporting to the Operations Officer, I was handed orders to escort a group of 48 P-47's from Karachi, India, to an upper Assam Airbase. The Operations Officer added, "They should be ready tomorrow morning."

I walked back into Goldwater's office where he said; "I've got the plane ready and have arranged for a party in Cairo, complete with belly dancers." I explained my orders to him and he said, "Those guys just got in from Germany. They have seen so much combat that they will not be in a hurry to get to the Burma front to fight Japanese zeroes; it'll take a week or two to get them out of here. You have time for a quick trip to Cairo, and I'm going with you or without you."

With the orders I had just received from the Operations Officer, I couldn't chance being found in Cairo, which was outside my theater of operations. I would be charged with being AWOL (Absent Without Leave), and for an officer, the punishment for that offense was severe.

The next day those P-47 pilots did not even make an attempt to leave Karachi. Every morning their escort was ready, but not the P-47's. Goldwater had been right! Those P-47 pilots were in no hurry to see combat again soon.

Goldwater was only gone a day or two. Our quarters were quite close, so upon his return, every afternoon was spent sitting, visiting and drinking his Old Crow whiskey. There was no ice, so it was just Old Crow and a little warm water.

Good whiskey like Old Crow was rare in India. At the time I never gave much thought to how Goldwater managed to find Old Crow in India, and it would be almost twenty years later before the truth would come out. By that time, he was a U.S. Senator for the state of Arizona, and I was in the aviation business training airline pilots. One night, while we were sharing a motel room in Greybull, Wyoming, with a bottle of Old Crow on the table between our beds, he told me the rest of the story.

Major Goldwater and Colonel Baker were good friends. They were both based at the Wilmington, Delaware, Air Base, and in the process of being transferred to India, Colonel Baker was to be the Commanding Officer of the Chabua Air Base in Assam, India, and Major Goldwater was to be the liaison officer for Crescent Airlines.

Crescent Airlines was a military airline that served the C B I Theater from Wilmington, Delaware, to India, by way of Azores Island; Casablanca, North Africa; and Cairo, Egypt. Prior to the defeat of Germany in North Africa, the air supply to India had to be routed by way of Miami, Florida; through Puerto Rico to Natal, Brazil; from

Natal to the Ascension Islands in the Atlantic; to Gold Coast Africa; to Cairo, Egypt; and then on to India.

Goldwater and Baker were together in Wilmington, when Baker made an arrangement for a fifth of Old Crow whiskey to be sent to him in Chabua, India, once a week, by way of military carrier mail on Crescent Airlines. Goldwater, as CBI liaison officer of Crescent Airlines in Karachi, India, was in charge of carrier mail. He would intercept Colonel Baker's Old Crow each week, replace it with India gin, and then send the gin on its way. That night I asked Goldwater if Baker had ever found out. He laughed and said, "We are still good friends, and he doesn't know to this day what happened to his Old Crow." I think Goldwater probably drank Old Crow without ice and with a little water for the rest of his life.

Every morning I would arrive at the flight line ready to takeoff along with the P-47's on the first leg of the flight to Assam, India, only to have the flight canceled. Finally on the morning of June 8, 1944, things appeared different. Everyone and everything seemed ready to go. It was an impressive sight, sitting in the B-25 with both engines running, looking down a long line of 48 P-47's as they all started their engines. We led the group to the runway and took off. The P-47's followed, taking off two at a time at 30-second intervals. They soon formed a large formation with the B-25 in the lead. It was something to see. At the time, there was no way of knowing that in a very few weeks, I would be flying a C-47 amid this group, as they were attacking the Japanese far behind enemy lines, deep inside Burma.

When we arrived in Agra, India, four hours later, things were going smoothly. A couple of days later we arrived at their new fighter strip near the India-Burma border. It was a temporary strip, made of stamped steel plates, located close to the fighting in the Imphal Valley, India, and Northern Burma. With the escort mission complete, we returned with the B-25 to Chabua Air Base.

During the trip to pick up the B-25 and escort the P-47's to their new base, the intense heavy fighting to save the Imphal Valley was concluded, as the Japanese had finally been defeated. Japanese Zeroes had shot down each of the two B-25 pilots who had left Chabua with me. Both were killed as they carried desperately needed ammunition into the Imphal Valley, after the Japanese had captured much of the British ammunition and then used it against them. Had the Imphal Valley fallen to the Japanese, the supply lines to all of

Assam, India, China and Burma would have been cut, releasing a large Japanese military force that had been tied down in China and Burma fighting for control of all of Southeast Asia. It is probable that this would have affected the outcome of fighting in the Pacific Theater.

CBI Theater

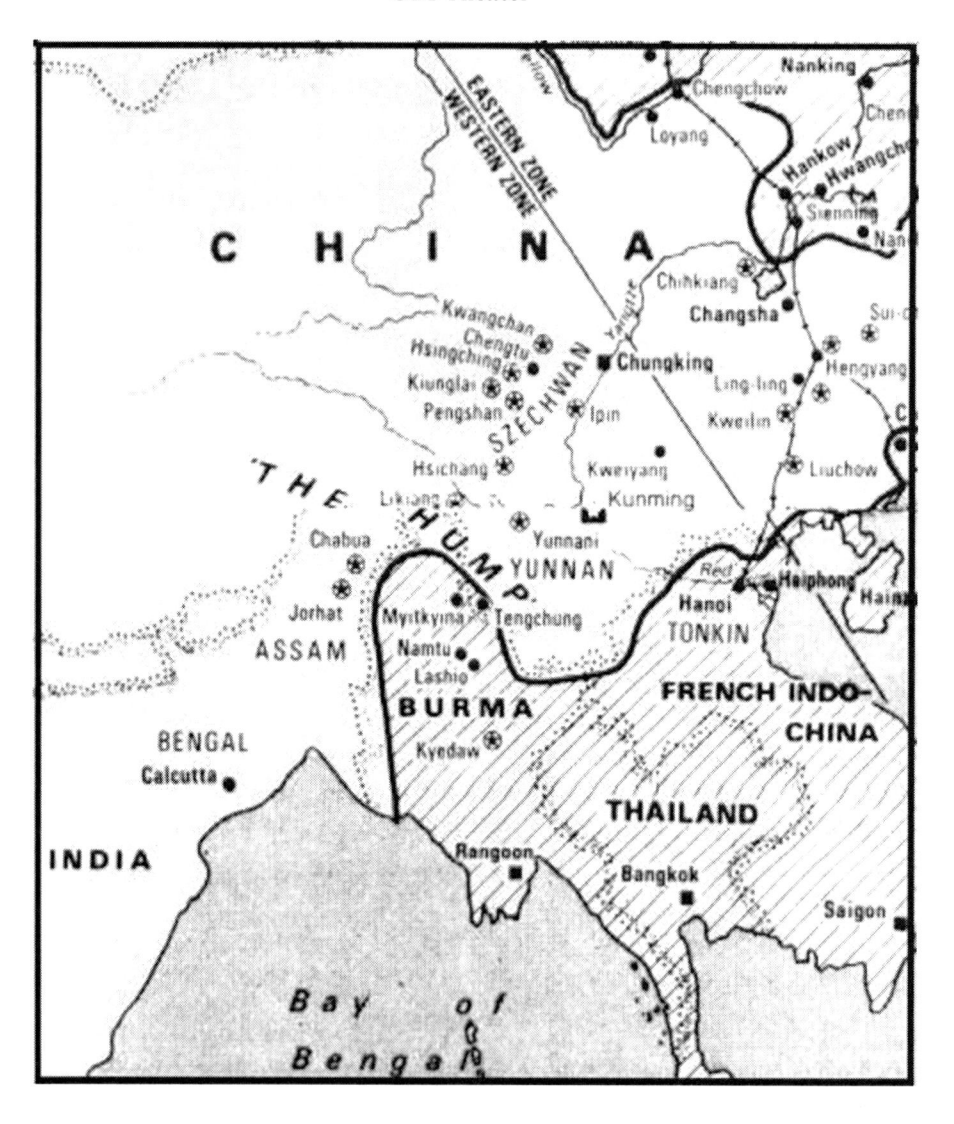

Chapter 20
803rd Medical Air Evacuation Transport Squadron

After returning to Chabua, I received a new assignment: The Operations Officer explained that I was being given a rest from Hump flying. He said, "You are assigned as 1st pilot on a C-47 hospital ship." What a break! Flying from Ledo Hospital in Assam, India, to Calcutta, would be a snap.

Loading Wounded Marauders

The C-47 was the same aircraft as the Douglas DC-3, the most popular passenger plane used by most airlines during that time period. Some also called it the "Gooney Bird", and the ground troops called it the "Dakota". The Troop Carrier Command used the C-47 for supply drops, parachute jumps, and glider towing. China National Airways, which was kind of an extension of the Flying Tigers, was using DC-3's and C-47's for passengers and cargo. The gross takeoff weight of a C-47 was about 35,000 pounds, compared to the 48,000 pounds of a C-46. They were both tail-draggers. When taxiing the C-47 in winds, I used the elevator and ailerons for directional control in the same way, as one would taxi a Piper J-3 Cub.

Being checked out on the C-47 hospital ship was no problem until the check pilot said, "Every landing must be perfect: no bounces, no skips." He explained that the medics would be working during landing, and a perfect wheel-landing was required. I indicated that perfect landings could not be made using this aircraft, and he said, "All you have to do is concentrate on the landing, and you can do it." He was right! For the first time, I realized how little attention was given to landing.

The next day was spent flying the local Assam Shuttle, a passenger plane connecting all the air bases in the Assam Valley. The monsoon season was in full force with unbelievably heavy rain, very low ceilings and visibility. While Chabua had a new low-frequency range station with two ADF's (Automatic Directional Finder) to align us with the runway, all other air bases used a single ADF for instrument approaches.

One instrument approach that day came very close to being a major accident. It was an ADF circling approach with low ceiling and visibility. While we were breaking through the clouds over the runway, a 270-degree turn was required to align with the runway in order to land. A very steep turn was made to prevent losing sight of the runway, and after reducing power, I made a landing. After touchdown, I felt as if some power was still on, so I kept pulling the levers against the stops and complained to the co-pilot. He replied, "You have the props, not the throttles." The prop and throttle positions on C-46's and C-47's were reversed. This was not a problem under normal conditions, but when under high stress, a pilot will subconsciously revert to old habits.

Normally, there would have been more than enough runway to come to a safe stop, but with the heavy monsoon rains, there was no braking action, and the plane continued to move down the runway. As the plane rolled past the end of the runway, each landing gear wheel struck a triangular runway end marker, which acted as a brake, quickly bringing the plane to a stop.

There was a 15-20 foot drop a short distance off the end of the runway. There we sat! The landing gear was only 3 feet from the edge, the cockpit was beyond the edge, and both engines were still idling. We asked the tower to send a tractor to pull us back to the runway. With the engines still idling, the tractor hooked to our tail wheel and pulled us backward to the runway. Once back on the runway, we taxied to the terminal. At the terminal we cut the left engine to let the passengers off and board new passengers. Then we restarted the left engine, taxied out and took off.

This incident demonstrated how three feet could make the difference between the total loss of an aircraft and a pilot's career, or a complete non-event.

On the next trip, we carried a load of sick and wounded from Ledo Hospital bound for Calcutta, India. The hospital ship carried 21 litters mounted on each side of the center aisle. We carried a medical crew of one doctor, one or two nurses and one or two medics. After completing this trip and having logged over 20 hours with 23 landings in less than a week, I was told, "You are ready for Burma, report for a briefing in the morning."

The assignment was to evacuate sick and wounded Merrill Marauders from Myitkyina, Burma. The briefing officer explained, the airstrip is 150 miles behind Japanese lines, surrounded and under fire with a mile-and-a-half perimeter. The airstrip lies in a northeast to southwest direction. Make your approach for landing as steep as possible to avoid ground fire. The southwest end of the runway is on the east bank of the Irrawaddy River. The Japanese hold the west bank. You can expect machine gun fire if you fly over the east bank. Today, you have good weather with broken clouds. Most of the time you will have to find a break in the clouds over the Hukawng Valley, then get down on the jungle floor, find the Ledo Road and follow it south. The Ledo Road becomes the Kamaing Road behind Japanese lines. Fly low and close to the jungle to prevent the Japanese from hearing the approaching aircraft. The Kamaing Road intercepts a railroad that will lead you eastward straight to the Myitkyina airstrip. When following the road or railroad in low visibility, always fly on the right side to avoid a collision. Troop carrier planes are using the same route to and from Myitkyina.

Arriving at the aircraft revetment, I was met by a doctor and two male medics. The female nurses were not taken on trips when flying and landing behind enemy lines because on the day following the capture of the Myitkyina airstrip, the hospital plane was strafed by a Japanese Zero. During the strafing, three of the medical staff were wounded, and an injured Marauder, whom they were loading, was killed.

As we entered the pilot compartment, the co-pilot explained that his friend was located in a bunker somewhere on the Myitkyina Airstrip. His friend was the air traffic controller, and the co-pilot wanted to visit him. It sounded much safer than staying with the airplane, so I agreed to go with him.

Air Evac C-47 Taking Off From Myitkyina
(A Japanese fighter had just strafed the airstrip, wounding a nurse and killing a patient. A Burmese laborer is lying dead in the foreground with new bomb craters in the runway. The C-47 took off after being shot up, which wounded three of the medical staff and killed a Marauder patient.)

The flight to Myitkyina was no problem, with a visual approach through broken clouds. As we turned onto final approach with full flaps, we used no power and a speed slower than normal to obtain a steep glide path. The traffic controller said, "All incoming aircraft circle northwest of the airstrip, and then clear the area for dive bombing and strafing." We pulled up and formed a circle with two C-47 troop carriers northeast of the airstrip.

Looking up high in the sky to the southwest, I saw twelve of our P-47's flying in echelon formation. We watched as one by one they peeled off at about 3-second intervals. It looked as if they were dive-bombing the airstrip. We could see the bombs release from under their wings, but as the bombs fell, they would travel further and further from the airstrip, exploding a mile or two away. After the last P-47 dropped its bombs, they started strafing the enemy, and we were cleared to land, while the strafing continued.

We were in the number one position to land. While on a steep final approach about 300 feet above the ground, we saw that a P-47 was coming at us in a shallow dive from about 45 degrees on our right. We could see his six wing guns firing. The rapidly blinking fire coming at us from each wing was a frightening, but exciting, thing to see. He passed under our aircraft. Looking down from the left window, I could see him still firing. Fire from his guns extended a foot out from his wings. With all twelve of our P-47's strafing all around, we knew we were in the middle of a war.

After landing, we taxied to the parking spot reserved for the hospital ship, parked and cut the engines. Immediately, we could hear gunfire and ricocheting bullets. Looking ahead to the other side of the runway, I could see the wreckage of aircraft and gliders. Stepping out of the airplane, I noticed something strange: nobody was paying any attention to the gunfire. Soldiers in ragged, dirty uniforms were unloading supplies off troop carrier planes, and the men were in pitiful condition. I had seen severe combat fatigue, but never anything like this.

The doctor suggested that we go with him to the field hospital, as it was the safest place around. We explained that we wanted to find the co-pilot's friend, and that after that, we would come to the field hospital. The doctor and the medics took off down a path that ran 90 degrees to the runway. After receiving directions, we started down the runway, looking for the bunker that housed the air traffic control.

We walked southwest, parallel to the runway, about 400 feet from our plane. Suddenly, a very loud explosion made the ground seem as though it jumped a foot. We both hit the ground, but to our surprise, no one else took cover or even seemed to notice the explosion. Those near us looked at us as though we were well-dressed dodo birds that were out of place, and we were. Pilots were trained to fight in the air and were completely out of their element on a battlefield. We had unknowingly walked over a bunker as a 105 Howitzer fired a round at the enemy. I told the co-pilot, "You go on. I'm going to do what the doctor said and find that field hospital." After getting on his feet he said, "I'm going with you."

Returning to the plane, we took off down the path, which the doctor had taken. While we were walking southeast down the path, side by side, a shell went by us. We both hit the ground. It exploded on the path about half-way between our aircraft and us. (One doesn't need any experience to recognize a shell when it passes.) The trajectory was so flat that, by jumping three feet and reaching out to the left, I could have caught it. After it exploded, we jumped up and ran to the left through the brush, looking for a slit trench. A second shell went over, and we hit the ground again, and we then got up to find a trench. As a third shell went over, we both saw a trench and dived for it. Curled up at the bottom of a 3-foot deep trench, only big enough for one person, we waited for the shelling to stop.

Finally, after a dozen rounds, the shelling stopped! I said, "I'll flip you to see who gets out to see if it's all over." His answer was, "The hell with you. I'm staying here." My response was, "Man, I gotta pee." He said, "Not in here."

Standing with only my right leg in the trench, and putting my left leg over the side, with my head still down in the trench, I thereby relieved myself, solving my problem. Suddenly, there was laughter. Looking up and behind me, I saw about twelve Chinese solders coming unglued, as if it was the funniest thing they had ever seen.

After that embarrassing experience, we returned to the path and proceeded to the field hospital. As we approached, one of Doctor Seagraves' twelve Burmese nurses met us, and in broken English said, "You come over to this side; it's safer." She then led us to a place in the three-sided dirt airplane revetment that offered protection from shellfire.

Doctor Gordon S. Seagraves was a medical missionary who had trained twelve Burmese nurses prior to World War II. In 1942, the Japanese invaded Burma, driving Seagraves and his nurses; General Stilwell and the Americans; General Wingate and the British; through Northern Burma into Assam, India. Seagraves was commissioned a Colonel in the American Army and became known worldwide as "The Burma Surgeon". He provided Stilwell's armies with field hospital facilities.

At Myitkyina, the field hospital was located inside the aircraft revetment. The three dirt sides of the revetment provided some protection from incoming fire from the south, and tents inside the revetment housed patients on cots. On one side of the revetment were some makeshift operating tables under a rusty corrugated tin roof. It was a busy place, full of sick and wounded troops. At sunset anyone who could fire a gun was taken out and put on the line to fight. After months of jungle fighting, the Marauders were all psychological casualties and plagued with malaria, mite typhus and amoebic dysentery, but for a Marauder to get evacuated, he had to be wounded and unable to fire a weapon.

As soon as the 21 patients on their litters were loaded, the co-pilot and I entered the plane and headed for the pilot compartment. The smell of rotting flesh was unbearable. We closed the door, opened the windows, and tried to keep the pilot compartment under positive pressure to get rid of the stench. We quickly started the engines, taxied to the northeast end of the runway, and took off. Remembering that Japanese guns were on the southwest side of the river directly in front of us, we made a steep 90-degree right turn as soon as the wheels left the ground. We climbed north before turning west toward Ledo.

During our short time on the ground, we experienced battlefield conditions and witnessed its results. The twelve rounds of shelling down each side of the runway killed 8 Chinese, 2 Burmese and 3 oxen. In the background, there was always the sound of gunfire and ricocheting bullets. The profound sympathy we felt for the Marauders blinded us to all the risk and hazards in getting as many as possible to the Ledo Hospital.

Immediately after unloading the wounded, we returned to Myitkyina for another load. After landing and parking in the same place, we got out of that hot airplane, while the wounded were loaded. Standing by the tail of our airplane, we watched the unloading of ammunition from a troop carrier C-47 parked next to us. A Jeep drove up, and a driver jumped out and started loading boxes of ammunition onto his Jeep. He wore no hat or shirt, his undershirt was torn, and his pants were baggy, dirty and torn. As he turned, we could see his insignia pinned to his pants at his belt line. This soldier was a full chicken Colonel.

Our plane was quickly loaded. We boarded, started the engines, and were just about to release brakes, when someone ran out in front of us, waving his arms. Looking back, we could see that he was trying to open the door. This Marauder had been hit by enemy fire while no more than 10 feet from the tail of our plane. We shut down the left engine so the door could be opened. He was laid on the floor by the door, and one hour later, he was in Ledo in an ambulance on his way to the hospital.

P-47 takes off to provide air cover while troop carriers unload.
(Myitkyina soon became a major air base, and its existence played a major role in the defeat of the Japanese in Burma.)

On later trips into Myitkyina, I was given mail to take to Doctor Seagraves. He was always found in the middle of surgery, at a makeshift operating table, working under very unsanitary conditions. On one patient, he had the abdominal cavity open, and on the other, he had made a large incision in the upper thigh. There were flies crawling on the open incision and the surgical instruments. He was doing the best he could, under battlefield conditions, because any internal bleeding had to be stopped. If these soldiers lived, only two things were certain: One, they would receive the Purple Heart; and two, they would be evacuated out from the battlefield to the Ledo Hospital.

Some of our trips were not behind enemy lines, but rather into unimproved landing strips near the fighting along the Ledo Road. One such trip proved interesting. After landing, we found the mud was so deep that it presented a problem. We used the engines to turn the plane into the loading area. The plane turned, but continued moving in the same direction, slipping sideways. Once the plane stopped, the patients on stretchers were loaded onto the plane. We could see that the landing gear wheel was buried in mud up to the hub, and getting airborne was going to be a problem.

After we started the engines and tried to taxi, we found that the plane would not move, even with full power. By dropping some flaps, applying full power, using the elevators to lift the tail, and with hard down elevator, we got the plane moving. As the plane moved down the airstrip, the elevators were used to get the wheels rolling on top of the mud, instead of in the mud, allowing the plane to quickly accelerate to take-off speed. Interestingly, it was the same technique I had learned in the late 30's to be able to take-off in snow, while flying Piper J-3 Cubs.

One day, after finding a hole in the cloud cover over the Hukawng Valley, and descending to the jungle floor, we flew south to intercept the Ledo Road. As we were following the road, heavy rain and low clouds reduced the visibility to almost zero. Suddenly, another C-47 flashed by on his side of the road. There were no more than 100 feet between our wings.

On another day, we were approaching Myitkyina over enemy territory, and flying just 3 feet above the flat jungle to prevent the Japanese from hearing the plane approaching. As we passed 90 degrees to a road cut in the deep jungle, a Japanese truck convoy was heading north, loaded with troops. Crossing the road, we got a good look at the Japanese troops sitting in the trucks. Not one enemy soldier looked up, which proved that they did not hear us coming.

Leaving Myitkyina, with a low overcast, we usually followed a railroad westward, and then a road northward. One day we took off from Myitkyina with a 400-to 500-foot ceiling and unlimited visibility, and followed the right side of the railroad track westward. Up ahead, three fires could be seen. Three columns of black smoke were rising into the overcast. We knew immediately that the Japanese had set guns on the railroad tracks, shot down three C-47's on the same course we were on, and that we were about to be the fourth. By making a quick climbing right turn to the north toward the mountains into the clouds and away from the Japanese guns, we avoided the fate of the other three C-47's. A few minutes later, we turned back to the west, continued to climb, and headed toward the Ledo Hospital with another 21 wounded and sick Marauders.

One morning in mid-July of 1944, we were assigned a hospital trip to Kunming, China, flying a C-46. Tied down in the center of the cabin floor was a cargo of medical supplies, and sitting forward of the cargo were a doctor and three medics. The weather was terrible, and it was raining. (It is impossible for anyone to realize how hard it can rain, until he has experienced a monsoon season in that part of the world).

We entered the pilot compartment, and it was agreed that I would be co-pilot going to China, and first pilot on the return trip. After taxiing to the runway, we made our run-up and started our take-off. After following the pilot's application of power, adjusting the throttles to proper take-off power and tightening the friction lock, I started a routine engine check. Suddenly, seeing and hearing the engine RPM increase, I realized that we had a run-away right engine. While I pointed to the engine RPM gauge, the pilot made the decision to cut all power and abort the take-off.

Looking up for the first time since starting take-off, I could see that we had more than one-half the runway remaining, and that the air speed had only reached 80 miles per hour. There was more than enough room to stop. However, it was raining so hard, leaving so much water on the runway, which a hydroplaning effect produced between the tires and the runway had left us with absolutely no braking action. It became apparent that we were going to go beyond the end of the runway. Knowing how much mud and water we faced, I had to take emergency procedures. I brought the mixture control to "idle cutoff", turned the gas valves to "off", unlocked the tail wheel lock, and yelled to the pilot, "Tail wheel unlocked; you had better ground loop the SOB!" The pilot applied full right rudder and hard right brake. There was no more than a 10-degree change in direction, and no apparent braking action, as we crossed the end of the runway.

The mud and water beyond the end of the runway provided quick braking action. The braking was so quick that the tail of the aircraft came up, allowing water to hit the hot engines, which caused white steam to obscure vision from the pilot's windows. There was also a loud crashing sound coming from the cabin area. Remembering the four passengers sitting in front of the cargo, I jumped out of my seat and headed for the cabin, just as the nose of the aircraft was coming up and the tail falling. Rushing into the cabin, expecting to see four injured passengers, I found nobody there. Then, from the tail area of the aircraft, the four came walking forward. The doctor had recognized the abnormal increase in the engine speed, and led his medics to the rear section of the cabin in anticipation of an accident.

Following the accident, a hearing was conducted. It was determined that the run-away engine had been caused by a malfunction of the electric propeller, and that there had been no pilot error involved. Had the pilot continued take off, a crash, killing everyone, was almost a certainty. Even if the malfunctioning propeller had been feathered, the aircraft of that day did not have the ability to continue take-off and fly-out on one engine.

This marked the end of the air evacuation business, and it was back to the Hump flights. They had said, "Flying hospital ships would be a rest from the Hump", but flying low behind enemy lines, landing and getting shelled in the middle of a lot of small arms fire, was not my idea of R&R.

Chapter 21
The Final Hump Trips

It had been seven weeks since my last Hump trip to China. What a difference seven weeks can make during wartime. The route to China was no longer behind enemy lines, so if a person had to bail out, he was not likely to be taken prisoner and killed. The Japanese airstrip at Myitkyina, Burma, had been captured, and that reduced the possibility of unarmed transport planes being shot down by Japanese zeroes. This also allowed us to fly directly from Chabau to Kunming, and new southern air routes were being established over lower terrain, away from those mountains that were 20,000 feet and higher. New low-frequency radio ranges were being installed in India and China. This provided better navigation and safer instrument approaches. Air traffic had gotten so heavy that air traffic control clearances were being used to separate aircraft.

Things were getting better on the ground, too. Fresh new pilots were arriving, and we saw fewer skinny, sunken-eyed, combat-weary pilots around. The required number of round trips for rotation back to the States was 65, and it was no longer being increased each month.

Thinking I needed five more trips to meet the rotation requirements, the Operations Officer helped me get them in fast. Round trips were made on July 14th, 15th, 17th and 18th. Just one more round trip, and I should get orders back to the States. On the 19th, just 3 hours before take-off, and thinking it was to be my last Hump flight, I received new orders. They transferred me, not back to the States, but to Karachi, India. I was very angry and upset; thinking only one more trip was needed before orders to the States would be received. The operations officer failed to tell me that I had completed the required 65 round trips, and he said, "In Karachi you are to check-out some pilots on C-46's, and then you will receive your orders to the States."

The assignment was to establish the CBI portion of Rocket Airlines, which was a military airline established to supply the 20th Air

127

Force. The 20th Air Force was flying B-29 super fortresses from their base in Calcutta to advance air bases in China. From China, they had the range to bomb Japan, but only after the necessary fuel and bombs were flown to their bases in China. The fuel was being carried to China in converted B-24 four-engine aircraft tankers. This sure beat the old way of carrying 55-gallon drums in C-46's.

After arriving in Karachi the next morning, I discovered that the aircraft to be used for checking-out new pilots was not airworthy. Things got worse when the Maintenance Officer said, "We are so far behind, and I can't tell you when we can do that work." After convincing him I was an aircraft mechanic, I was given box of tools. I fixed everything but the landing gear. Working on the landing gear required aircraft jacks and the use of portable hydraulic power. The Maintenance Officer said, "It will be three weeks before we can schedule you to use the jacks." My reply was, "We can't wait three weeks. We will take it up and troubleshoot the problem in the air." It worked! Tracing the hydraulic system in the belly of the plane, and tapping on a one-way check valve, I got the landing gear to work. After replacing the check valve, we started checking out pilots.

Another pilot was assigned to help, and we kept flights going around the clock. It didn't take long to get the job done. When the check-outs were complete, I asked for orders to go home. They said, "You are not done. You have to route-check them." So, we preceded to route-check them from Karachi to Calcutta and back. After the route-checks were completed, I once again asked for orders to go home. They said, "You will have to fly as line pilot until you receive your orders."

Every day, an hour or so was spent in Karachi Air Base Personnel Office, asking for my orders, while quoting personnel regulations from memory, and even making up a few of my own. With every trip to Calcutta, a stop was made at the CBI Wing Headquarters Personnel Office, asking for my orders to go home. Survival was now dependent, not so much upon flying skills, but upon hope, a bottle of paregoric in my pocket to control diarrhea, and the wish that orders to the States would come soon.

My last trip on Rocket Airlines was on Sept. 28, 1944. We had a 0800 departure time, but the aircraft did not check-out. By 1700, we were checking-out our 5th aircraft, and everything checked-out except the fuel flow gauge. It showed almost twice the normal fuel flow.

Assuming the fuel flow gauges were faulty, we decided to ignore the problem and take off for Calcutta. After just passing Agra, India, the Flight Engineer said, "We don't have enough fuel to reach Calcutta." Upon calculating fuel used, we found that the fuel flow gauges were right. No one could understand how the engines could have used that much fuel. We needed to get the aircraft on the ground. The radio operator called Agra, India, and advised them of our trouble and that we were going to land at Agra.

After landing at Agra, we taxied up to the transit ramp, parked, set the brakes and cut the engines. A Jeep came racing up to our plane. It was the Agra Air Base Maintenance Officer. Before the props stopped, he was in the cockpit with us, saying, "We can't handle your problem here. We are going to top your tanks and you will fly on to Calcutta." My reply was, "Major, if you want this damn airplane to go to Calcutta in this condition, you will have to fly it yourself because I will not."

At that point, the Major came unglued and angrily said, "Captain, you will fly this airplane to Calcutta tonight, or I will file court martial charges against you." With equal anger, I said, "Major, you might as well start your court martial, because I'm not going to fly this damn airplane until it's airworthy." He then ordered me to get into the Jeep with him and said, "I'm sending you back to Karachi, and I'll start your court martial first thing this morning."

It was a little after midnight. As we approached the Operations Office, the Major told the Operations Officer, "Put this pilot on the first flight to Karachi." The Operations Officer said, "There is a cargo plane leaving in about 45 minutes." To really make matters worse, I said, "No, Lieutenant! When does the first plush-cushioned passenger flight leave for Karachi?" His answer was, "It leaves at 0600 in the morning." This was the breaking point for the Major, as he ordered me to take the cargo flight. Turning to the Operations Officer, I asked, "Lieutenant, what priority do I have?" He answered, "You have a number two priority." My next question was, "Will that get me a seat on the passenger plane?" His response was, "Yes." With that answer, it was off to get a little sleep before the flight.

The first pilot on the passenger flight to Karachi was Captain Earl G. Adams. He had previously taken me to the British Officers' Club on the beach in Karachi, and we had become good friends. The trip was spent in the cockpit telling Earl about the run-in with the

Major. The court martial didn't seem to worry Earl, but then again, nothing ever worried Earl. I was too sick to care. That morning after arriving in Karachi, we walked into the Karachi Operations office, and the Operations Officer gave me the news that my orders to go home had been received.

Chapter 22
Orders Home

From the Operations Office, it was straight to the Personnel Office to pick up orders, then to my quarters to pick up my B-4 bag, and then to the passenger desk to catch a flight. They got me on the first plane to Cairo, Egypt, and I spent the next hour inspecting the aircraft to make sure it was airworthy. After getting this far, it didn't make any sense to get killed going home.

The pilot gave us a grand tour of the Holy Land from the air, as he circled the Dead Sea, Jerusalem and Bethlehem. My statement to the Chaplain sitting next to me was, "We probably should spend a week seeing the Holy Land, since we are here." He was a Catholic Priest, and his statement was surprising: "No, I've been there, and you are better off seeing it from here. This way you don't have to deal with the stench. There had to be better people living there during the days of Christ."

In Cairo, they told us it would be one or two weeks before we could get any further, and instructed us on how to get billeted. Hearing this, I set my B-4 bag in front of the passenger desk, sat on it, and waited for the next flight. It worked! After about 45 minutes, the sergeant at the passenger desk came over and said, "Come on. Let's see if I can get you on this plane to Casablanca." He did, and it was an unforgettable trip.

Our flight was over the North African desert, where the great battle against the German and Italian Nazis had just been fought. Looking out the plane's window presented a sight never to be forgotten: War debris was scattered over the desert for hundreds of miles. It was impossible not to wonder what had become of my old B-25 outfit. They were the 486th squadron of the 340th bomb group, and we had been in advanced combat training at Walterboro, South Carolina. I had served as squadron flight leader throughout the combat training, and was briefed for a flight to join the invasion of North

Africa. Just twenty-four hours before departure, the flight surgeon had found I had a hernia, and I was taken to the Columbia, South Carolina, Army General Hospital. The rest of the squadron went on to North Africa, and very few of them survived the war.

Casablanca was a very busy terminal, and nobody knew how long it would be before anyone could catch a plane to the States. There was a baby aircraft carrier leaving for New York, and they encouraged everyone to take it. If sitting on my B-4 bag in front of the sergeant's desk worked in Cairo, it should work in Casablanca.

Later in the afternoon, after everyone had left, and feeling that my plan had failed, I saw an officer come into this large empty terminal. He said, "Are you still here? Come on; let's see if we can get you on this C-54 before it leaves." I grabbed my B-4 bag, ran out the door, and jumped into his Jeep. We raced down the ramp to a C-54 that was just starting its number 4 engine. He pulled up in front of the plane and waved to the pilot. Then he drove around to the door. It opened, and I tossed my B-4 bag onboard. They then dropped a knotted rope, and I climbed up into a plush-cushioned passenger plane - on my way home at last.

The flight was from Casablanca to Miami, Florida, with a quick fuel stop in the Azores Islands. I took a commercial airline from Miami to Little Rock, Arkansas. This completed a trip over half-way around the world in less than two days and back home to a new wife and a new red Chevrolet.

Part III

Crop Spraying, Aerial Contract Spraying and
Airline Pilot Training School

CHAPTER 23
ATC Ferry Command 1944

What is it like to return home after being in a combat area for months, and living in a bamboo basha with a group of pilots? Many times we would come back to our basha and find an empty bunk and a pilot's foot locker gone. We would know we had lost another pilot, but it was easier to think, "Well, he has gone on a trip, and he's not coming back." It served us well to not get to know our basha mates on a personal level. Nevertheless, the stress builds up. After months of living under those conditions with poor food, in hot and humid weather, and carrying a bottle of Paregoric to fight diarrhea, we could end up very skinny, with our eyes sunk back into our heads, due to the loss of essential body fat. Looking back, that was the way it was, but at the time we were in a state of denial, which was probably good for a faster recovery.

It was great to be back with my new wife, my new, red 1942 Chevrolet and good food. My orders read, "Report to the Adams Field Army Air Corps office in Little Rock, Arkansas." On my first day home, I reported. When the sergeant saw that I was only three days out of India, he said, "You haven't had time to get here, so come back later, and we will start your leave time." About a week later I was back in his office, and he said the same thing. At the end of two weeks, I was ready to get back to flying and asked for orders. My orders read, "Report to the Wilmington Army Air Base in Wilmington, Delaware." So, my wife and I took off in our new, 1942, red Chevrolet, with a national speed limit of thirty-five miles per hour, using a special gas rationing book.

At our new base we were provided a nice apartment in the married quarters. The Army Air Corps provided link trainer time and gave me a green card. Only a very good pilot could receive a green card, as it allowed him to fly in or out of an airfield that was closed due to weather. I was ready to fly, and thought about how good it would be to have good weather reports, a great air traffic control system, and good instrument approach systems. No longer would I be flying behind enemy lines and have to worry about enemy fighters or navigation stations being jammed. I could hardly wait to get back in the sky.

Finally, at the end of November, I got orders to ferry a new C-46 from the Curtis Aircraft factory in Buffalo, New York, to Memphis, Tennessee. My co-pilot and I left by high-speed train to New York City. When we reached New York's Grand Central Station, we went to spend the night with the parents of my co-pilot. They lived in a beautiful high-rise apartment with a large picture window overlooking New York's Central Park. The next morning we were off to Buffalo by train, and arrived to find real bad weather. The weather was below minimum, and the field was closed, but with my green card, I filed an instrument flight plan. The new C-46 had been de-iced in a warm hanger and had been moved out of the hanger by the time we arrived. We started the engines and released the breaks, but the aircraft would not move. Water had gotten into the wheel brake system and frozen.

It didn't take long for the mechanics to solve the brake problem, and by 2300, with both engines running; we were taxiing for takeoff with only 500 to 1000 foot visibility. All we had to do was find the end of the runway. When we were on the runway in takeoff position, we could only see two or three runway lights. Normal procedures were to takeoff and circle the field for twenty minutes. If everything was okay, the Army Air Corps owned the airplane, but in this weather there would be no circling the airport. We climbed to our assigned altitude of 8,000 feet, heading west on the airway leading us to Detroit. At 8,000 feet we were still on instruments, and everything was normal for the first forty minutes, but then the right engine started cutting in and out. After a few minutes of trying to fix the problem, I feathered the prop, called Detroit Radio, and declared an emergency. They gave us a clearance for an instrument approach into Detroit City Airport. The weather was ceiling 400 and visibility one mile. After receiving this clearance, I remembered being a passenger on another instrument approach into Detroit City Airport. I'll never forget stepping off that DC-3 and looking up at the very tall gas storage tanks on both sides of the runway. After refusing the clearance, they came back with a clearance to Fort Wayne, Indiana, with a ceiling of 400 feet and visibility three miles. We made a normal instrument approach into Fort Wayne, but when we saw the runway, the tetrahedron showed the wind blowing from the right into our dead engine. Applying full power on the left engine and asking for lights to be turned on the other runway; we made a tight two-hundred and seventy degree low left turn and landed into the wind. It was about 0200. With full 2000 horse-power at high RPM, under a 400 foot ceiling and over a populated city, it must have caused a real disturbance.

At Fort Wayne we were given orders to go to Buffalo to ferry another C-46 and deliver it to Mobile, Alabama. My copilot and I arrived in Buffalo in the afternoon, and the same weather system had the field closed. I had not fully recovered from that last flight and had no desire to ever use my green card again. We checked into a downtown hotel. That evening, dressed in our Class A uniforms, we had dinner at a table next to the stage, and after dinner I ordered a stinger for an after-dinner drink. The floor show started, and an Indian magician came on stage. He was greeted by loud applause, and having just come from India, I shouted something in his language at him. He appeared not to hear me. He was very good, and suddenly he came to our table. He took us both onto the stage and sat us down in chairs. We were then part of his show and he was using us to pull all kinds of magic tricks. He turned to my co-pilot and said, "You have a baby chick in your coat", and sure enough, he reached into his coat and pulled out a two live baby chicks. He then said, "You also have one in your pants." My co-pilot stood up and started undoing his pants to get the baby chick out, but the magician stopped him and told him to just reach into his pants and get the baby chick. Everybody was laughing! I was laughing so hard that it closed my eyes, and suddenly I realized that I was the only one still laughing. Opening my eyes, there he was, standing in front of me, looking down. He said, "What are you laughing at?" How he got the baby chicks into my coat and pants, I'll never know. We returned to our table to find six after-dinner drinks on our table. Everybody wanted to buy us a drink. After that experience and all the after-dinner drinks, we were ready to go out on the town.

We left the hotel and headed down the street and into the first bar, where once again, we became part of a show. As I entered the bar, someone tripped me, and I fell to the floor, but this good-looking girl beat me to the floor, and I lay there on top of her. I got back on my feet to a loud, laughing crowd in the bar. After one drink on the house, we continued on down the street and came to a large dance hall with a big band. We entered the dance hall just as they were ready to start a jitterbug contest. A girl grabbed my co-pilot by the arm and led him to the stage. The band started playing, and my co-pilot was the winner. His prize was just what we needed most: a bottle of champagne.

The next morning the weather was still instrument weather, but it was above minimum, and I didn't need my green card. We filed an instrument flight plan: Buffalo, New York, to Mobile, Alabama. They were forecasting a front moving into Alabama, but it was expected after our estimated time of arrival. We took off and were clear of the clouds in about twenty minutes. We had clear weather, but there was a pretty good head-wind slowing us down. After passing Atlanta, Georgia, which was our alternate airport, I become concerned about that front moving toward Mobile, because on reaching Mobile, we would only have twenty minutes' fuel left. Halfway between Atlanta and Mobile was our point of no return to Atlanta. After checking the Mobile terminal weather, where it was reported clear, and with the terminal forecast in our favor, we were committed to landing in Mobile. About ten or twenty minutes before reaching Mobile, we went on instruments and then started our instrument approach. This airplane had a radio altimeter, the first one I had ever seen, and I asked the co-pilot to set it to four-hundred feet and to call out the readings. After passing low cone of the radio range station and descending, the co-pilot yelled "400!" I said "Set to 300". He yelled, "300!" Just as we reached 100 feet, still on instruments, I saw a smoke stack go by my left wing. I raised the nose and applied climb power. We broke out of the clouds where we could see the runway ahead and to the left. It would take a 30-degree left turn to line up with the runway. The problem was that we went right back into the clouds, but with the correct bank angle, we broke out of the clouds with the runway lights directly in front of us. There was just one more problem: a red blinking light that was above the runway lights. We cleared the tower and landed safely on the runway. In the Mobile operations office, I was complaining about the poor weather forecast, while they were telling me that my orders were to fly another C-46 to Memphis, Tennessee. By this time it was pitch dark outside, and the full force of the cold front had unleashed its fury on Mobile. After dinner, the weather had settled down. It was instrument weather all the way to Memphis, so we filed our instrument flight plan from Mobile to

Memphis by way of New Orleans. When we got to Memphis, about 0200, I told operations that I was sick and was going back to Wilmington. By 0800 that morning I had used my high priority and was sitting on a DC-3 airliner, heading home at last.

On December 13, 1944, I was co-pilot on a new British B-26G from the factory in Baltimore to Nashville, Tennessee. My first thought was about all the B-26 pilots being killed while training in Lake Charles, Louisiana, and we called that airplane "The Flying Coffin". The pilot said that he had 800 hours in the airplane and had just returned from England. While he had a lot of combat experience, he had no experience flying airways. We checked the weather together, and it was instrument weather all the way to Nashville. Nashville had a 400 foot ceiling and moderate icing. I said, "I'll file IFR (Instrument Flight Rules)." He said, "No! File VFR (Visual Flight Rules)." I should have refused to make the trip, but when we walked out to the plane, I said "There is just one thing I want to know about this airplane: What is the bailout procedure?" He showed me how to release the entrance hatch. We took off and headed west, and everything was going well until we came to the Appalachian Mountains. He was trying to find his way through cloud-covered mountains, and I said "Take her up." He paid no attention to me, so I got up out of the right seat and started adjusting my parachute when he asked, "What are you doing?" I said, "I'm leaving you." He said, "OK! I'll take her up." We started climbing through the cloud cover and finally broke out on top at 11,000 and proceeded to Nashville. A new problem was that the airplane had no low frequency radio, only very high frequency. It was the first one I had ever used. Actually, I had never heard of this radio. We were VFR on top and couldn't talk to anyone to file an IFR flight plan, but we kept trying. Finally, as we got close to Nashville, they answered and instructed us to maintain VFR on top in a holding pattern. To make things worse, all traffic had been stopped for over an hour, while they were trying to locate us. We were then at 13,000 feet where they left us for forty-five minutes while they got traffic moving again. I used this time to review the instrument approach procedure for the pilot. With an indefinite ceiling of 400 feet, moderate icing, and an airplane without any deicing equipment, I said, "You have to make it on your first approach because we are going to have a good load of ice, and I would not want to climb back up through it." By that time, I did not trust the pilot or the airplane. I talked him through the complete approach, and we landed with just a small amount of ice.

When I returned to Wilmington, orders were waiting, sending me to Miami, Florida. What a break: getting out of the very cold weather, and I'd had enough experience with the ferry command. Just four deliveries and three were scary enough to equal my Hump Pilot experiences. So my pregnant wife and I loaded up our 1942 new, red Chevrolet and headed south. We followed the coastline route all the way to Miami, FL, observing the thirty-five mile-per-hour speed limit.

During the last week of 1944, while we are on our way to Miami, the Battle of the Bulge was being fought, General Patten's army and allied forces were making advances toward Germany, and it was felt that victory in Europe was in sight. There were only three air supply routes to the European Theater of War. The northern route was by way of Greenland to England; the U.S. east coast to Casablanca by way of the Azores Islands; and the southern route by way of Miami; Natal, Brazil; and across the Atlantic. Two routes also carried supplies and personnel that were going to China, Burma and India. Eastern Airlines had the Miami to Natal, Brazil, contract route.

CHAPTER 24
Eastern Airlines 1945

Eastern Airlines had run out of pilots, and military pilots were being loaned to Eastern to fly one of their military contract routes. We would be flying C-46's from Miami to Natal, Brazil. Eastern was located at the 36th Street Airport, and as I reported to their office, the first thing I heard was, "On this route we have no weather cancellations." After almost a year of flying that flight, I had never heard of a flight being cancelled because of weather.

I was surprised at how many Hump Pilots were assigned to fly for Eastern. During this time, I ran into Earl Adams, my good friend I knew from India. We both were complaining about the high cost of rent in Miami. He knew I was heading for the Officers Club. He said, "If you think rent is high here, wait until you get to the Officers Club. They get 50 dollars a month for dues." I came unglued and was mad as hell, and said, "To hell with them. I'm not going to pay that for dues." Then, as I walked into the Officers Club office, I said to myself, "Cool it, let them speak first." I asked the sergeant, "What are your dues?" He said "Captain, for our officers it's five dollars a month, but for new officers with Eastern, it will cost you nothing." Earl had tricked me, but to save money, we ended up sharing a very nice home with him and his wife, near the airport

Earl Adams had 2100 hours first-pilot time in C-47's, but no C-46 time. He did not make first-pilot with Eastern, so I got him assigned as my co-pilot. It worked out great. A round trip took four days. Eastern Flight 6 left Miami each night at 2300, and landed in Puerto Rico at 0420 for fuel and breakfast. It departed Puerto Rico at 0520, and flew direct to Georgetown, British Guyana. We spent the night in Georgetown, departing early the next morning for Natal, Brazil, with a fuel stop in Belem, Brazil. After an overnight in Natal, we spent the next two days returning to Miami. On each round-trip we logged close to 40 hours of flight time.

Our flight crew included a radio operator and a navigator. These long flights could get pretty boring, and for something to do, I would compete with the navigator to see who could shoot a three-star fix and compute our position the fastest. One night, I wanted to see how close our navigator could get us to the end of the Natal, Brazil, runway, using only celestial navigation. He provided me with heading and altitude; and using no other references, he was only off a quarter-mile from the end of the runway.

The efficiency of the airline was amazing. We even adjusted our power to arrive on time, and most of the time, while on final approach, we would see another Eastern plane taking off or leaving the traffic pattern. Aircraft maintenance was perfect, and whenever we pulled up to the terminal, a mechanic was there to ask us if we had any maintenance problems. Once, I had a cylinder head temperature gauge that didn't work on the left engine. Fifty-five minutes later, when we started the engines, it was working.

Earl and I worked out a very good system: I would fly left seat the first and third day, and he would fly left seat the second and fourth day. Each evening we would have dinner together with one drink, and then, the one flying left seat would return to the barracks and get a good night's sleep while the other would hang out at the bar and have a few more drinks. We were on our return trip home, and I had flown left seat from Natal to Georgetown, so it was my night to have a few more drinks. But, as we were having our drink, Earl ran into a couple of old friends. By the time I finished my drink, I looked down the bar to see two or three drinks in front of Earl, so I headed for our room to get all the sleep I could before a 0230 wake-up call. Our room had bunk beds, and I took the lower bunk. Later, I woke up to find two of Earl's friends doing their best to get him into the top bunk, fully dressed. As they left, turning out the light and closing the door, the door opened again, and a hand reached in and turned the light back on and called, "On flight." I got up, walked over to the sink and turned around just in time to see Earl getting out of the top bunk, thinking he was in the bottom bunk. When he hit the floor, the entire building rocked, because it was on ten-foot posts to keep it off the jungle floor. With the help of the staff car driver, we took him to the airplane and laid him in the right co-pilot seat with his seat-belt fastened. Thank goodness, it was very dark, and no one could see us. The driver took off, and I went to flight operations to do the paper work. Then I went back to the airplane and waited for them to call the flight. The flight was called and after they loaded thirty-six passengers, I started the right engine. This woke up Earl, and as he rose up, he pulled the gear handle to the up position and hollered, "Gear Up!" He immediately went back to sleep. I put the gear handle to down position and was thankful that the gear-down safety lock was working. As I was taxiing, we hit a bump, and the jar woke Earl up again. He tried to raise the landing gear again, but this time I held it in the down position, and he quickly lay back down. When I applied takeoff power, the loud roar in the cockpit woke up Earl and he grabbed the gear handle and said, "Gear up." I had to hold the gear handle down with my right hand and the yoke with my left hand, and keep the plane going down the runway with my feet. As we lifted off, I released the landing gear handle. Earl raised the landing gear and lay back down in the co-pilot seat, and didn't wake up until 1000 that morning. I swore that, never again, would I be in the cockpit with a drunken co-pilot.

Earl was spending all his free time looking for a yacht to buy, and since he was the biggest trickster in the country and had tricked me once already, I decided to trick him. On our next flight, I made up some fake weather reports for Puerto Rico terminal weather, and got the radio operator to help me pull off the trick. We took off from Miami on schedule at 2300, and after climbing to cruise altitude, I laid my seat back, leaving the flying to Earl, and made out like I was asleep. About an hour out, just past Nassau, the radio operator said to Earl, "Miami radio called, and it sounded like they were asking us to return to Miami, but I can't make contact with them." Earl woke me up, and repeated the whole story, and asked me what to do. I said, "We are already this far, so let's go on to Puerto Rico". Then I lay down and pretended to go to sleep. A few minutes later, the radio operator handed Earl a weather report. Earl reached up and turned on the ceiling spotlight to read the report. With a very loud voice, Earl said, "Damn! Look at this weather for Puerto Rico: ceiling 500, visibility 1 mile, wind 76 miles per hour, heavy rain, approaching hurricane. This is the reason they wanted us to return to Miami. Let's turn around now and return to Miami." I said, "Let me see it." He folded it up, put it in his pocket, and said, "I'm going to keep this and show my friends back in Toledo what kind of weather we had." I said, "Earl, if we continue another forty-five minutes, we will be past our point of no turnaround for Miami, and we will have to land in Nassau, where you can look for boats all day." That was music to Earl's ears, and I got up and went back to the navigator's desk where I started writing weather reports to bring the weather to normal. I gave these to the radio operator. By the time we reached our turnaround point, the weather looked pretty good to Earl. As we turned onto final approach, letting down over the ocean, everything looked normal, and on landing rollout, I said to Earl, "It doesn't look like a hurricane has been here." Earl didn't say anything, so I assumed he knew it was a joke. A little later we were in the operations office, filing the next flight plan when I suddenly realized Earl was not with me. Rushing down the hall to the weather office, I saw Earl and the weather officer with the weather report in his hand. As I walked into the room, the weather officer was saying, "Captain, we haven't had any weather like this in over two years. There has to be an enemy sub sending this out. I'll get intelligence on this right away." As I walked into the room, he was reaching for the phone, so I quickly said, "Wait a minute; it was all a joke." From the look on Earl's face, I knew there was big trouble ahead, and I had to be on guard all the time.

Soon after that trip, we were called to make a trip in an Eastern DC-3 from Miami to Havana, Cuba, and return. He flew it over, and as I was flying it back, I told him that I had to go use the toilet. The air was glass smooth as I walked back to the rear of the plane. I had a feeling that Earl was going to pull a trick on me by jerking the control and sending me into the air, while using the toilet. I closed the door but held the latch in open position, and I put one foot against the wall. I was ready to get out fast, if he tried anything. Suddenly, I felt the elevator move, and I shot out of the door. I'll never forget floating next to the ceiling, looking up the aisle, with twenty-one passengers looking back. He had them buckled in their seats, and all were wise to the joke. While I escaped completely clean, the toilet was one holy mess. That airplane had left New York that morning and had been flying all day. The chemical toilet had never been serviced. Now its contents were thrown all over the toilet. After closing the door, I went to the cockpit and said, "We are going to be in a lot of trouble when they see that toilet; it would be a good plan to not be available for a couple of days." Normally, it took about twenty to thirty minutes to do the paper work after a flight, so we decided to do all the paper work before we landed. When we parked at the terminal, the first two off the airplane were Earl and I. We walked by operations, tossed our paper work on their desk, went out, got in our car, drove to Earl's new boat, and cruised out to a beautiful key island lagoon. After anchoring, we swam to the shore and brought a couple of coconuts back to go with our rum and Coke. Shortly afterward, I was on the fan-tail fishing, while Earl kept diving down under the boat. On our last two trips, he had complained about his engine running to hot, and little did I know that he was setting me up for a dangerous trick. Earl said, "I think something is stopping the cooling water. See if you can use your finger to check the intake hole." Earl showed me where to find the water intake hole, and over the side I went. The visibility was very good, but under the hull it was pitch dark. Running my hand back and forth over the bottom, I finally found the intake hole. I was almost out of air, but I thought I'd give it one poke and then go up for air. Earl had the water pump going, and when I ran my finger into the intake hole, the suction grabbed it. I pulled, but it wouldn't come out. Then I thought that I might have to leave my finger in the hole, but I had to go up for air. With my knee against the hull, I gave one frantic jerk and went for air. When I finally opened my eyes, there was Earl hanging over the rail, laughing his head off. He had gotten even, but I still had all my fingers.

Earl made first pilot and we made no more trips together. I got a new co-pilot who had been a primary flight training instructor, and this was the first time he had been in a large aircraft. We left Miami at 2300 and climbed to cruise altitude. Then, as usual, I laid my seat back and went to sleep. Soon, the navigator woke me up, saying that the co-pilot was not holding a heading. I watched for a while and saw that he was going around every cumulonimbus cloud. I told him, "We don't have fuel to go around clouds; you have to hold the exact heading. I've been flying this route for months and have found that you don't even have to slow down for these thunderstorms." On the next leg of our flight, which was from Puerto Rico to Georgetown, there was always a stationary front just past our point of no turn-around. The front was ninety degrees to our course, and it formed a line of violent looking thunderstorms with lightening as far as we could see. I said, "We are not even going to slow down, and I'm going to prove to you that it is okay to fly through cumulus clouds." We experienced some mild turbulence and some Saint Elmo's Fire on the props but nothing like I had experienced flying the Hump. The next evening, after refueling in Belem, Brazil, as the sun had set and it was getting dark, we were climbing to cruise altitude, and ahead was the worst thunderstorm I had ever seen. My new, inexperienced co-pilot said, "You are going around this, aren't you?" I said, "No, we can't change course." As we got closer and closer, it looked much worse, and I slowed down to a speed that would limit the G-load to a maximum of two G's, and dropped the landing gear. For the next three to five minutes, we experienced the most violent thunderstorm I had every flown through. My new co-pilot said, "I thought you should have gone around that one." He still didn't understand that when you come to a line of storms, you either go through at ninety degrees to the line of storms or turn around, and on Eastern, you didn't turn around.

There was one trip, on July 12, 1945, when we were returning to Miami, and due to head winds, we only had twenty minutes' fuel reserve, and at the Miami airport, weather was ceiling zero and visibility zero. We had no choice except to make an instrument approach, using the low-frequency range. Using time and rate of descent from low cone to the end of the runway, the first thing we saw was the end of the runway at only fifty feet. Very soon after landing, I was getting very sick, and in about twelve hours after landing, I was in the Army General Hospital in Coral Gables. They were treating me for a psychological problem caused by that zero-zero landing. Then, my pregnant wife arrived at the hospital and delivered a baby girl. She was just one floor above my floor, and she got out of the hospital before I did. A month after that landing, I got back on flight status and logged seventy-five and one-half hours by the end of August.

A call from Eastern operations informed me that I was being assigned to the Miami to New York flight, and to come to their office at 0800 in the morning to prepare for the trip. As I left home the next morning, I told my wife that I would be home by noon. After spending the morning studying the airways, approach charts and holding procedures, I thought I knew it all, but after an Eastern pilot questioned me he said, "Keep studying." It was 1700 before they were satisfied, and at 2100 that night, the phone rang and I heard, "You have the midnight flight to New York tonight." By 2300 that night, while filing my flight plan, I said to the co-pilot, "We have three fronts to go through, and we will be on instruments all the way." By the time we reached cruise altitude, we were passing through our first front. That night our ground speed changed so much that we were constantly off on our estimated time of arrival over the next radio range station.

After passing Roanoke, Virginia, Air Traffic Control kept stepping us down until we were at minimum instrument altitude and just west of Washington, D. C. Air Traffic Control told us that the traffic was so backed up in New York that we would be landing at Washington, D.C., National Airport. They cleared us into a holding pattern on a marker beacon about twenty-five miles west of Washington, D.C. We were in a thunderstorm, and after forty-five minutes, I called Washington radio and explained our problem, and they cleared us for a straight-in approach. After parking the airplane, I got out of my seat, lay down on the floor of the airplane, and went to sleep. Around 1000, someone came aboard the airplane, woke me up and said, "You are cleared to New York, La Guardia airport." We were on instruments all the way, and after landing at La Guardia, we went over to Manhattan and checked into a hotel across the street from Radio City Music Hall. Later, we walked a very short distance and had dinner at the famous Toots Shor's Restaurant. The next day we flew back to Miami with no weather problems. After one more uneventful round trip to New York, I was back flying the Miami – Natal flight.

On one trip, we had taken off from Belem, Brazil, in route to Natal, when a passenger sent word to the cockpit that the right engine was leaking oil. I checked the oil pressure. It was normal, and I sent word back that it was not unusual for there to be some oil on the wing. Soon the passenger sent word that I had better take a look, so I went back and looked out his window, and he was right: there was oil running over the wing. It was not long before the oil pressure started dropping. We feathered the right engine and radioed Natal, telling them about our problem, and that we were changing course for Fortaleza, Brazil. Fortaleza was about one hour short of Natal. We had a hard time holding attitude, and slowly drifted down all the way to Fortaleza. On final approach, I could see an Eastern C-46 that was turning north toward Miami. That C-46 had brought a mechanic from Natal to fix our problem, and he was standing by a fuel truck near the runway. When we rolled to a stop, the mechanic started fixing our oil problem, while another man was replacing the lost oil. Very soon, the mechanic came aboard with his tools, and we were off for Natal, arriving only one hour late, and the airplane departed on time for Miami. It was amazing how efficient this airline operation was. The Army Air Corps could really take some lessons from them.

In the beginning, our flight always left Miami for Natal with a maximum gross load of 48,000 pounds. The war in the European and Pacific was being fought, using maximum effort. We were winning in both theaters of war, and Hitler's Army was defeated by the end of April, 1945. After their defeat, we were flying back from Natal to Miami with a maximum load of 36 passengers. Then on August 6, 1945, the atomic bomb was dropped, and we knew that Japan was defeated. Had it not been for the atomic bomb, the invasion of Japan could have cost well over a million lives.

Shortly before the defeat of Japan, I was asked to accept orders sending me to California to flight-test the new jet fighters. This would mean a career in the Army Air Corps. My wife and I talked it over and decided not to accept the offer. A couple of weeks later, they asked again, and once again, we talked it over. This time we decided to accept the test pilot position. It was the afternoon of August 6th, 1945, when I headed to the airport to accept the orders. While driving to the airport, down 36th Street with the radio on, I heard a news report that Bong's jet had blown up in California. We had been in the same class of 42D at Luke Field, Phoenix, Arizona, and had graduated together on April 24th, 1942. It was a shock to hear this news. His death changed my whole life, because I made a 180 degree turn on 36th Street and went home.

Richard Bong was a famous Ace who had shot down forty Japanese aircraft while flying P-38's in the Pacific War. We both had been awarded the Air Medal and the Distinguished Flying Cross, but Bong was awarded the Medal of Honor by the President of the United States. While Richard Bong's death made all the headlines, there were many test pilots killed who did not even make news in the local papers. It is ironic that on the same day of Bong's death, the first atomic bomb was dropped on Japan. Days later, the second atomic bomb was dropped. Japan unconditionally surrendered, and World War II was over. After contributing so much to the defeat of Japan, it's too bad that Bong did not live long enough to see the end of this war that had lasted almost four years.

When the Japanese surrendered, things changed fast: billions of dollars of contracts were cancelled, and millions of servicemen would be discharged over the next year based, on their time in service. Since I had been in the service before World War II, I was ordered to Barksdale Field on October 19, 1945, and separated October 31, 1945.

My wife and I returned to Little Rock, Arkansas, and faced the big question of what to do then.

American Airlines had promised me a pilot job as soon as I was separated from the Army Air Corps, but I felt that I was not healthy enough, and flying co-pilot for years was not appealing. Next, I had the opportunity to sell surplus war material. The first deal was two or three train-loads of 100-octane aviation fuel and a boxcar load of eight day clocks. This had all the signs of a crooked deal, with payoffs all the way back to Washington, D. C. I left that deal fast! A close family friend of my wife's family was a doctor with a surgery practice in Kansas, and he wanted me to go to medical school and take over his practice, because he wanted to retire. After completing all required pre-med courses with straight A's, I was accepted into the University of Arkansas Medical School. Near the end of my first year, I joined the doctors' medical fraternity. That gave me a close look at the life of a doctor, and it was not good. Being a guest in their home for dinner, I saw that they were nearly always interrupted to go to the hospital. While I enjoyed the curriculum, that regimen was not the way I wanted to spend my life. I bought some land, build a small home, subdivided the land, built more houses and became Herrod Construction Company. A wise old real estate man said, "You are building high quality cracker boxes. What you need to do is get into large expensive homes." I did, during history's worst winter. The housing market crashed, and I went broke. I took a job as pilot on a feeder airline; it lasted a few months and ended when a major airline took over the route. Some friends talked me into going crop dusting, and this venture lasted for the next fourteen years.

CHAPTER 25
Crop Dusting 1948

The crop dusting business was not new to me, because I had spent a few summers, before the war, working as a flunky mechanic. For a pilot, crop dusting was a very dangerous business, with a two-percent loss each season, and a season only lasted sixty to ninety days. I would study each accident in great detail to find what the pilot had done wrong, and what would have been the correct thing to do to avoid the accident. This experience contributed to my next fourteen years in the aerial agriculture business, flying without an accident or even a scratch on an airplane.

It was the spring of 1948; I headed to Helena, Arkansas, to become one of "Terry's Pirates", as the crop duster pilots were known. Terry had leased the large hanger that had been used by the Army Air Corps. He was buying surplus Boeing-Stearmans and PT-17's that had been used in War II for primary flight training, and converting them to crop dusters and crop sprayers. He was leasing the aircraft to pilots, and the pilots got thirty-percent of the gross. He paid for the fuel and maintenance, and the pilots paid their own travel expenses. A pilot could make three-to-five-hundred dollars a day, which was very good money in those days.

Crop Dusting in the Mississippi Delta

A crop duster's day started at the very first sign of dawn. We would takeoff and fly across the Mississippi River, landing in the Mississippi Delta, on a crop duster strip. The plantation manger would show us the cotton fields that were to be dusted. Calcium arsenic was used as an insecticide on the cotton. Calcium arsenic is a powder, and as everybody knows, arsenic is a deadly poison. By the time we returned to the airstrip, both the pilot and airplane were covered with calcium arsenic dust. Most of the veteran dusting pilots believed that chewing tobacco would keep the arsenic out of their system. They told me how to kick the rudder to make the air slice across my face, while I spit the tobacco juice. I tried it once and decided to take my chances with the arsenic.

Cotton fields in the Mississippi Delta sometimes have power lines running across them, and we would have to fly under them. A good duster pilot knows that he has to work under power lines at close to ninety degrees, and he doesn't look at the wires, but he looks at the power poles. If the power poles make a turn, there is going to be a guy wire there that can take a wing off. If a pilot hits the power line, it will break, but it he hits a high tension line, he is not likely to survive. Many cotton fields are surrounded by tall trees, and since we must fly only one or two feet above the cotton, our pull up has to be timed perfectly to make our wing downwash force the dust into the cotton and still miss the trees. We kept dusting until the sun started heating the ground, which caused the dust to rise. Then we flew back to Helena to have breakfast.

After a good breakfast, I would get back into the plane and fly north into rice country, to spend a few hours sowing rice or fertilizer. We would arrive at the strip to see a semi-truck and trailer loaded with one-hundred-pound-sacks of rice seed or fertilizer, and our first thought would be, "How long is it going to take to unload that truck?" Things go fast when sowing rice seed or fertilizer. The landing strips were very close to the flooded rice fields, and we would be spreading over one-hundred pounds of fertilizer per acre, and carrying six-hundred pounds per load. We timed our output so we could open the hopper door when we reached the field. Then, when we made our turn at the far end, we closed our hopper door, while heading back to the strip. With two loaders, it would only take a minute or two to load, and then we would be back in the air. After a few hours, we would be heading back to Helena in time to get a couple of loads of dust on the cotton before the sun set.

    A new herbicide came on the market, and it was very effective in killing broad leaf weeds. The wheat fields in the northern states were losing much of their yield because of weeds. So with a newly converted spray plane, I took off for Grand Forks, North Dakota, and sprayed a thousand acres of flax. Each night we would call Helena to report our location and receive instructions as to where to go next. At that time, long distance telephone calls were handled by live telephone operators, and they got to know all the pilots. If we wanted to know where another pilot was, all we had to do was ask the telephone operator. Next, I was sent to Minot, North Dakota, and from there to a very small German immigrant community. They all spoke German and didn't trust any outsider. Their wheat fields were full of weeds, and some fields were a bright yellow, because of the mustard weed. I spent a week trying to sell my service, but no one believed me. Finally, one farmer said, "You can spray this forty acres; it is lost already." The next day, the field that had been a bright yellow started changing color, and after a few days, the field was a beautiful dark green. For several days, we could see cars and pickups parked on the road next to the field, and farmers out in the field inspecting the results. Soon, they all wanted my service, and I spent the next two days turning down jobs because the wheat was in the boot stage, and we were not supposed to spray. The boot stage is when the grain kernel is forming. I flew back to Minot and waited for my next spray job. I did not have to wait long. My next job was to spray 734 acres of wheat, west of Minot. When the farmer and I sat down to settle up, he said, "I'm paying you for 350 acres." I said, "No, get out your maps, and we will add up the acreage. The amount of chemical used was 735 gallons, and we apply one gallon per acre." He got the maps, and it added up to 733 acres. After this farmer tried to cheat me, and with my bad experience in the German community, I wanted to leave North Dakota, so they sent me to Malta, Montana.

    It was about five o'clock in the evening when I landed in Malta and tied my airplane down. A friendly man gave me a ride into town. Malta was an old, small western town with an old western hotel, and most of the farmers were original homesteaders. Then I checked into that old western hotel and told the man behind the desk, "I've been flying that open cockpit airplane all day, and I'm going to have a drink at your bar before going to my room." I sat down on a bar stool among a group of total strangers. I'll never forget this drunken cowboy, who looked like Will Rogers, hanging on my shoulder, saying, "I just sold a whole truckload of wild horses, and they didn't bring hardly anything. You know what's wrong with those damn wild horses? They are just too much like humans; they do it for fun, and its wrecking hell out of the prices." Before I was half-way through my drink, more drinks were coming. Everybody in the bar wanted to buy this new stranger a drink. This was my first experience with real western people. They were honest and friendly, and would help anyone who needed help. Their word was their bond, because you could depend on it. They accepted my word and advice without question. They were the real salt of the earth, and I didn't know then that I would be spending the next thirty-one years in Montana.

Malta was having a terrible mosquito problem, and I offered to spray the town with DDT. First, the chemical tank had to be cleaned of the weed-killer and this was done by filling the tank with kerosene and taking off and spraying it through the boom. While flying about a hundred feet off the ground and spraying the kerosene, I looked back and saw a white cloud following the airplane. My first thought was that the airplane was on fire. Undoing my safety belt, I cut the power, stood up in the cockpit, and was going to jump out, but first I wanted to see flames. I could see no fire, so I dropped back into my seat, pulled back on the control stick, and landed in a small field. To prevent running into a fence, I hit the left rudder and brake, causing the plane to ground loop, while I jumped out and ran away from the airplane. When I looked back, I saw kerosene pouring from the airplane. A two-inch hose had come loose, and it only took a few minutes to fix the problem. I took-off and flew back to the airport and sprayed Malta. That ended the mosquito problem that year. This one experience may well have saved my life. Let me explain: A pilot plans for every possible emergency by practicing the proper procedure until he has the ability to subconsciously react properly to the emergency. For years, I could think of nothing worse than burning in an airplane, and I thought that it would be better to jump out. It was time to readjust my emergency thinking. Instead of jumping out of the airplane, which would result in certain death, it would be better to stay with the plane and be prepared to fight the fire.

One night there was a knock on my door. It was a farmer for whom I had just sprayed for a few days prior. He said, "You did a good job of killing the weeds, but it looks like you also killed the wheat." I asked him what stage of growth the wheat was in, and from his description, it was in the boot. I told him that when the wheat is sprayed in the boot, it will recover, but with some loss in yield. He said, "I have another three-twenty (320 acres) for you to spray in the morning." Think about it for a minute. Here is a man who walked into my room, thinking that I had killed his wheat and he listened, took my word, and based on my word, he had the rest of his wheat sprayed. Those were my kind of people. After promising everybody that I would be back the next year, I left for Arkansas. Once back in Little Rock, I stayed busy giving flight instruction, but there was no money in it. I could make more money spraying wheat in one morning than I could make in a month teaching flying.

Arriving in Helena, Arkansas, to start the 1949 season, and knowing my plans to return to Malta, Montana, they asked me to go to Fort Benton, Montana, because their growing season was well ahead of Malta's. I was off to Montana, flying across Arkansas, Kansas, Nebraska, and Wyoming and onto Billings, Montana, for an overnight stay. The next morning, I headed for Fort Benton. After a fuel stop in Lewistown, I was flying in the rain, under low clouds, following a railroad that ran straight toward Fort Benton. I went by a small town with a landing strip on the southeast side and a cemetery at the end of the runway. The wide main street was only four or five blocks long, and I could see muddy tracks in the dirt street. At the northwest end of the street was a train station and two or three tall grain elevators. I remember thinking, "Who would live in that pile of mud?" Little did I know that on that rainy day, I would spend the next eleven years living in Geraldine, Montana!

Fort Benton was a beautiful historic town on the Missouri River where Lewis and Clark passed on their trip that opened the western USA. The first people to settle Montana came up the Missouri River by steamboat, and Fort Benton was as far up the river as they could go. A stagecoach provided access to areas beyond Fort Benton. There were still stagecoach stops visible, and one of my customers' father had owned two stagecoaches that ran from Fort Benton to Lewistown. One day we went out to the Arrow Creek

Breaks, and he showed me the old trail where we could still see the stagecoach tracks.

My stay in Fort Benton didn't last long. Before leaving Arkansas, I was told that I would be doing all the spraying for Holman Aviation. Once arriving in Fort Benton, I found that they were going to do their own spraying. Since it was too early to go to Malta, I got in my airplane and flew twenty-five miles back to that muddy town. I checked into the very old, western, Geraldine Hotel. From the hotel, I walked to Rusty's Bar and started looking for wheat to spray. Like Malta, most of the farmers in the Geraldine area were homesteaders or the family of homesteaders, and they kept me very busy spraying wheat. After a few weeks of spraying in Geraldine, I knew that I had clientele for a very profitable business. After servicing my Malta customers, I made it back to Helena in time to do some more crop dusting.

Late one evening, after hours of dusting cotton, I landed at a Mississippi Delta Airport and was fourth in line to fuel. The airplane just ahead of me was a very old Travel Air. They were built in the early 1920's, and there were very few left. It was said to be one of the best crop duster aircraft ever built. It was dark by the time I fueled and tied down my airplane and I did not see the pilot of the Travel Air until we were inside under lights. When he took off his leather helmet and goggles, I saw a very old, white-haired man. This seventy-year-old duster pilot was one of the first duster pilots, dating back to 1921-22. The first dusting company was Delta Dusters, which later became Delta Airlines. A few years later he was killed, dusting in a new Piper. His death reinforced my firm belief that I would not stay in the business past the age of forty.

The year, 1949, was a good year; I not only had enough customers in Montana for a good business but I also ended the season with enough money in the bank to start a business.

CHAPTER 26
Aerial Agriculture Business 1950 - 1953

My philosophy has always been: "The only reason to work for someone else is that they know something you need to know, and they can teach you what you need to know." By using my aircraft and engine experience, and in my spare time helping convert Stearman PT-17's into spray planes, I had acquired the know-how to convert my own spray plane. After two seasons of saving money and building a customer base in Montana, I was ready to start my own business.

In the fall of 1949, with over five-thousand dollars in the bank, I paid four-hundred dollars for my first airplane (a Stearman PT-17) and spent the winter converting it to a ninety-gallon spray plane, and still had enough money to get it, my wife, and two very small kids to Montana. We were very low on cash but managed to buy food until the first of the month. Then, with no money left, I opened a charge account at the grocery store. It was a very late growing season in 1950, and the spray season was a good thirty days late. Although Geraldine had dirt streets, it had a nice-looking bank, so I went in to ask for a loan.

The old banker was sitting at his desk. I said, "Mr. Carley, I need seven-thousand dollars to buy chemical and be ready for the spray season. I am out of cash, and I still owe five-hundred dollars on medical bills back in Arkansas. I also owe seven-hundred- and-twenty dollars on my car, which is only worth about three-hundred dollars. My spray plane is fully paid for, but there is no insurance on it. It could get blown away, or I could have a crash, but if everything works out as I think it will, I'll have everything paid off and have eighteen-thousand dollars in my account in ninety days." To my complete surprise, he pushed paper across his desk and said "Sign there!" This was truly an old western bank, run by an old western banker. To me, they were the greatest people who had ever lived, and I was proud to live a few years among them.

Ninety days later, all my debt was paid off. We owned a new 1951 Chevrolet, a new thirty-six foot Travel-Lo trailer to live in, a two-and-one-half ton truck, and we had nineteen-thousand dollars in the Geraldine Bank. We went back to Arkansas for the winter, to rebuild the airplane by replacing the 220 HP engine with a Pratt and Whitney 450 HP engine, and to install a one-hundred-forty gallon chemical tank.

Stearman PT-17 being rebuilt in El Dorado, AR

In Little Rock, Arkansas, I bought a surplus BT-13, for its engine and prop, and paid three-hundred-and-twenty-five dollars. I took everything to our rented hanger in El Dorado, Arkansas. After months of hard work, the day of the first test flight came. I was thrilled at how fast the airplane jumped into the air, and the rate of climb was unbelievable. After testing the high speed stalls and doing some acrobatics, I started testing power-off stalls, but when moving the throttle forward to apply power, nothing happened. With the engine idling, I made a forced landing, to reach the parking area in front of our shop. With the engine still idling, I waved my mechanic helper to come over. When he saw me move the throttle forward, it was the first time he knew something was wrong. We both had failed to safety the nut holding the throttle linkage to the carburetor.

El Dorado, Arkansas, was the home of Murphy Oil Company, and my longtime friend, Bill Miller, was the company pilot for Murphy Oil. We were both in our teens when we spent one summer, back in the nineteen-thirties, working without pay, learning aircraft mechanic skills. I'll never forget the day he brought the two Murphy brothers into my shop to show them my airplane. One of the Murphy brothers said, "I don't know why you are going to all this work. You should go back to Montana and buy oil leases in the Williston Basin area. You can make a lot more money." I knew they were giving me good advice, but I also knew that with this new spray plane, and with the spraying to be done in Montana, I could make thirty-thousand dollars by midsummer. One year later, the headlines in all the newspapers read, "OIL DISCOVERED IN THE WILLISTON BASIN". I could have been buying oil leases for ten-cents an acre, and they became worth a thousand dollars an acre. A year after the oil discovery, I was having dinner with Bill Miller and the two Murphy brothers, at the Northern Hotel in Billings, Montana, and I said, "If I had done what you suggested, I would be a multimillionaire today." One of the Murphy brothers said, "It's not too late. Just go up to Wolf Point, Montana, and start buying." Later, I found out that in the first twenty-one oil wells they drilled in the Wolf Point area, twenty were double producers, and they knew that one was going to be a dry hole before they drilled it. So much for 20-200 hindsight!

Stearman at Geraldine, MT airport

In the early spring of 1951, it was time to head north for Montana. After spending the night in Casper, Wyoming, the temperature was at freezing and not suited for open cockpit airplanes. Taking off to the south against a strong south wind and with more than twice the horsepower the airplane was designed for, I was more than five-hundred feet high by the time I was half-way down the runway. Feeling the cold air in the open cockpit and with no traffic in sight, I made a steep one-hundred-and-eighty degree left turn and headed north for Sheridan, Wyoming. At Sheridan, while servicing the airplane, two Wyoming State policemen came up and said, "We have a warrant for your arrest for not following the Casper traffic pattern." I kept servicing the plane, started the engine, taxied out, and took off to the west. Two minutes later I was in the state of Montana, headed for

Lewistown, Montana. I never heard any more about it. Apparently, they were following the old western custom of not following a fugitive across the state line.

With my wife and two small children settled in an apartment at the Geraldine Hotel, it was time to get ready for the 1951 spray season. With a one-hundred-and-forty gallon chemical tank, there was no need to be flying out of pastures and having a tank truck following me around over dusty or muddy roads. Every load could be flown from the Geraldine Airport, so I built a loading station with an underground aviation gas tank, with a pump, meter and hose. An above-ground, large diesel tank, with pump, meter and hose, was connected to a chemical measuring system. The chemical measuring system was made with an old ten-gallon measuring glass with a hand pump to fill the glass tank with chemical. Getting around talking to farmers using ground transportation was a real problem; a person would wear out a new car in ten-to-twenty thousand miles. To solve this problem, I bought a 62 HP Aeronca airplane, and was landing on roads and pastures to talk to my customers. Baby-sitting my small son was something else. I would put him in the back seat, and off we would go. When he stood up beside the back control stick, he was tall enough to see out the window, and while standing with one hand on the stick, he could do a good job flying the plane. When a kid starts flying airplanes at the age of three years old, he is likely to become a very good pilot, which he did.

During the summer in Montana, we could start spraying as early as 0430, but we had to quit round 0900 in the morning. Later in the day, we could get an hour or two in just before dark. One evening I was killing time, waiting for the temperature to cool down. The old man who owned the Geraldine Hotel was sitting on the front steps, so I stopped to visit with him. Just for the sake of making conversation, I looked up at the front of the old hotel and asked, "What do you want for this old hotel?" He said, "Forty-two thousand." I laughed, and just for conversation, said, "I would give you twenty thousand for it." He said "Sold." Living by the philosophy that my word is my bond, I had just bought an old hotel that I didn't need and didn't want, but would own and operate for the next ten years. After making ourselves a nice apartment and using the old hotel dining room for an office, we made more apartments, leaving only a few rooms left to rent.

As the spray business kept expanding, we added another spray plane, and by 1953 we had three working. It was then that we had the first and only fatal accident. I had been in my office working with a customer when one of the spray planes had taken off to spray a wheat field that was on the north side of the Missouri River. Where he was to spray, the river ran through a very steep canyon. Suddenly, a strange feeling hit me. Being very disturbed, I was walking back and forth in the office for forty-five minutes, and finally the phone rang. I knew it was bad news even before I answered the phone. It was the Chouteau County Sheriff, and he said, "Your airplane has crashed and burned, and the pilot was killed." I can't explain my intuition. It was not the first time it had warned me of trouble, and it would not be the last.

CHAPTER 27
New Piper PA-20 1953

In the summer of 1953 I bought a four-place Piper PA-20, and had to go to Lock Haven, Pennsylvania, and pick it up at the factory. While I was in my office, making airline reservations, Chappel Rogers came in to pay for his spraying, and said, "If you take me with you, and on the way back, stop in North Carolina and let me visit my Mother, I'll pay all the expenses." Chappel Rogers was one of the first homesteaders to homestead in this area of Montana. In all the years of wheat farming, he had been no more than thirty-five miles away from his homestead. It was a trip I'll never forget. When I ordered food, he always said, "Make mine the same." We flew from Great Falls, Montana, to Pittsburg, Pennsylvania, the first day; and on to Lock Haven, Pennsylvania, early the next morning. We picked up the new PA-20 and flew to North Carolina. We landed at an airport near where his mother lived, and rented a car. Following a country road, we drove down a long valley. We came to an old frame house, and there was his one-hundred-year old mother, sitting in a rocking chair on an open porch. It was the first time they had seen each other since he left to homestead in Montana. A few days later, we headed home and stopped in Memphis, Tennessee, to refuel and have lunch in the terminal. We had to walk some distance, and the temperature was over a hundred degrees, and my friend was wearing his long underwear. We spent that night in Conway, Arkansas, with my parents, on their farm, and flew back to Montana the next day. For the first time in many years, this homesteader had discovered a world outside the Montana Missouri River Breaks. It was only a week later that he took the airlines back to North Carolina, but this time he flew to Seattle, LA, and then east to North Carolina. When he returned, he brought me a gift. It was a jug of North Carolina moonshine.

The four- place Piper changed our world. My wife, two kids and I flew to Arkansas to visit my parents, and to California to visit my wife's parents. I started attending aviation meetings of the

National Aviation Trades Association, and taking an active part in things affecting agriculture aviation. This led to my working with Donald Nyrop, who, at that time, was head of the Civil Aeronautics Board, and who later became president of Northwest Airlines. There had been no federal regulations governing agriculture aviation until now. We saw to it that when the Federal Aviation Regulation (FAR-Part 5) was finished, it didn't change a thing. We could still do anything we wanted to do to our aircraft, and fly it where and when we wanted to.

A family photo with our PA-20 in Conway, AR

The National Aviation Trades Association was promoting the development of an airplane for agricultural work. I flew my PA-20 to Bryan, Texas, to spend the day with Fred Weick, who was an aeronautical engineer in charge of the Texas A&M Aeronautical Department. After visiting their very large wind tunnel, and watching them test what would become the space shuttle, we had lunch with the Bryan Rotary Club. We had a long conversation about his work with Piper Aircraft and others. He would later work for Piper Aircraft at their Vero Beach, Florida, facility, developing the Cherokee and other aircraft.

On another trip to Texas, to meet with Bell Helicopter, I landed at Fort Worth airport, where Bell Helicopter sent a helicopter over to fly me to their factory. It was my first ride in a helicopter. That evening, I was the guest of the Cross-Country News Magazine and was treated to dinner at the Fort Worth Press Club. These visits led to a feature story about the development of agriculture aircraft.

Grumman Aircraft Company developed the Ag Cat, and on one of my trips, I was asked to flight-test it and make an evaluation. It was a bi-plane and had all the good characteristics of a top performer. The high speed stall recovery was much better than any spray plane I had ever flown. Little did I know then, that some fifty years later, at a

Quiet Birdman dinner, I would be sitting next to Corky Meyer, the man in charge of the Ag Cat development for Grumman Aircraft. He was a Grumman Test Pilot for years and ended up as CEO of Grumman Aircraft Company. His book, "Corky Meyer's Flight Journal" by Corky Meyer, should be a must-read for people in aviation.

CHAPTER 28
Aerial Agriculture Corporation 1957

Working with the National Aviation Trades Association provided the big picture of how the aerial agricultural business was expanding. New agricultural aircraft and new agriculture chemicals were coming on the market. Not only was the demand for aerial service growing, but the government was starting to let large spray contracts.

My entrepreneurial philosophy is that when you find a situation like this, and if you love and enjoy the work, it is time to get into, and/or expand your business, but only if you have, or can obtain, a complete knowledge of the business. Plan on three to five years of fast expansion, and consider exiting the business within ten years. By that time, the business will have matured, and competition will have limited its growth and reduced profit margin. The government will have new regulations to control your business, and lawyers will have increased your legal liability exposure.

My spray season was only lasting about sixty days, and then the aircraft would sit idle for ten mouths, so why not find a way to increase efficiency by moving the aircraft to other areas that had different seasons? A good entrepreneur will always try to increase the use of assets to obtain greater profits.

After filing for a Montana corporation and selling some stock, I sent an airplane and pilot to the wheat country just west of Spokane, Washington, to set up a new business. Their spray season started ahead of Montana's, but as we would soon learn, it overlapped, and we had to bring the airplane back or risk losing some of our Montana business.

When the Montana season ended, I sent an airplane and pilot to Greenville, Mississippi, to develop a Mississippi Delta service. I moved my family to Denver, Colorado, and rented an office in Denver's downtown financial district. With a new secretary to take care of the office, we were ready for business, and it didn't take long.

One afternoon, an executive of a top chemical company walked into my office. He asked, "Can you put enough large spray planes together to spray three million acres?" I said, "Yes. I just recently inspected about a hundred surplus C-105 flying boxcars that can be bought very cheaply. All I have to do is put in a thousand-gallon tank, and a pump, and hang a spray boom on the wing." He said, "We have developed a new insecticide and have been trying for over a year to get the Department of Agriculture to accept our chemical, but they refuse to even give us a try. We have reason to believe that they are being bought off, and we have people tracking both the government and the chemical company people."

Within the first fifteen minutes of being in my office, he had already received two phone calls and found out who the chemical company person was who was taking an airline to Washington D.C., and when that person would arrive. He also found out the name of the Department of Agriculture person who was meeting him. My office had become a call center for their covert operation.

He was staying in the hotel across the street from my office building, and he asked if he could use my office for a few days. That evening he was still in the office when I left to go home. During the night, I started to realize just how big of a deal this was, and how much money it would take to put it all together. Adding it all together blew my mind.

The next morning, he was already in the office when I arrived, and the first thing I said was, "I've been adding up the cost of this spray job, and I only have about thirty-five thousand dollars in the bank." He said, "Don't worry; we will deposit a hundred- thousand in your account to start with." All day long, he kept receiving phone calls from his intelligence network while I spent the day making plans to convert flying boxcars into spray planes. The following day it all came to an end. The Department of Agriculture agreed to give them a very large acreage to test their insecticide. As he left the office, he said that he would give me a very low price for his chemical. This really made me a lot of money during next few years.

A short time later, a man from New York City came into my office and said, "A friend of mine told me that you are trying to expand your aerial application business. I own controlling interest in a company listed on the New York Stock Exchange, and our stock has been dormant for a couple years, and I need to take some action to get it moving." After discussing who the biggest companies were, and how they would fit together, he said, "If you will get a five-year financial history, and an option to buy them, we will see if we can put it together."

In the office building across the street was a law firm with about twenty lawyers, and in the same building were the offices of a nationwide accounting firm. After explaining everything to each of them, they both agreed to help me put it together at their expense. It was understood that they would get our business if we were successful in forming the world's largest Aerial Application Company. With all the ducks lined up, I went to Denver's Stapleton Field, got into my airplane, and was off to Phoenix, Arizona.

My first stop was in Phoenix, AZ to visit Morris Aviation. They were the largest agricultural aviation business in the country. To my surprise, the manager had been my civilian ground instructor back in 1941, as a cadet, at Thunderbird Field in the Army Air Corps primary flight training. They gave me a room at the beautiful Sky Harbor Motel located on the airport. I'll never forget my first evening there, while sitting near the swimming pool. On the other side of the pool were several black men having drinks. One of them came over and invited me to join them for a drink and to attend something they were going to that evening. Being raised in the South, I politely declined. The next day I learned that they were the famous Mills Brothers, and they were performing somewhere in Phoenix that night.

After a stop at an operator airfield a few miles north of Sacramento, California, my next stop was Walla Walla, Washington. Evergreen Aviation was using helicopters, and they gave me a demonstration ride that scared the hell out of this fixed-wing spray pilot. At the end of a spray run, the helicopter pulled-up, stopped, turned one-hundred-and eighty-degrees, and then dove back into the field to make the next spray run. Fifty years later that little spray company would grow into the world's largest multipurpose aviation company. They would also build one of the best aviation museums in the country. It is located in McMinnville, OR. It became the home of Howard Hughes' "Spruce Goose".

My next stop was in Missoula, Montana, home of Johnson Flying Service. They developed the forest fire smoke jumper service, and were leaders in using planes to fight forest fires. They had a fleet of large TBM's, three Ford Tri-motored spray planes, and a valuable

Air Carrier Certificate. I had known Bob Johnson for several years, and his company had overhauled my airplane engines. He offered to sell Johnson Flying Service for seven-hundred-and-fifty thousand dollars.

By the time I returned to Denver, all hell was breaking loose. The Mississippi operation was in trouble. The man, who had built the spreader for rice seeding, knew how to get rid of a new competitor: by building the hopper to spray the rice unevenly. We would end up getting sued by the farmer. Next, word came that a bank had purchased Morris Aviation, and that Johnson Flying Service had been sold. Some big money expanded the operation located north of Sacramento, by creating an operation in Australia, which, being in the southern hemisphere, provided a year-around business. It was one exciting winter, but it was time to close the office. I returned to Montana, gave the investors all their money back, closed the corporation, and got ready for a new spray season. My work in Denver had made one thing very clear: Operators bidding government spray contracts were doing very well, and I had no trouble getting on their bid list.

CHAPTER 29
Government Contract Spraying 1957 - 1961

After a very successful wheat-spraying season killing weeds, we had a grasshopper infestation. Not only were we using the new insecticide to save wheat crops, but the U S Department of Agriculture's Bureau of Land Management (BLM) was asking for bids to spray large acres to kill grasshoppers.

Bids were sent by Western Union, and spraying outfits sent their bids back by Western Union. The successful bidder was notified by Western Union, and he would receive a phone call from the project manager. Then things moved fast: we had to order chemical and diesel oil, and move airplanes, trucks, and equipment to the job sight.

One of our first government jobs was on the Fort Belknap Indian Reservation, south of Harlem, Montana. We had moved our tanks, pumps, and other equipment onto an open prairie. The Indian chief was running a grader, preparing a landing strip for us to use. His six kids were running all over the place. He stopped, came over to collect his kids, and said, "My kids are acting like a bunch of wild Indians." It was getting late, and as we were getting ready to leave, he said, "You'd better spend the night guarding this equipment, or those tanks might not be here in the morning." So we set up camp and guarded the landing strip until the job was completed.

The next big bid was to spray a large acreage on the Rocky Boy Indian Reservation, east of Box Elder, Montana. The bid was immediately cancelled, and we were told that they were going to use their own airplane to spray. Later, I was passing the Box Elder air strip and saw about twenty government cars and trucks and one spray airplane. I stopped and said to the man running the job, "It would have been a lot cheaper to have accepted my bid." I'll never forget his reply. He asked, "Tom, haven't you been around long enough to know that when working for the government, you get ahead by how much you can spend, not by how much you can save?"

Converted twin engine Beechcraft at Great Falls, MT

To help the government spend more money, I spent the winter modifying two twin-engine Beechcraft spray airplanes to add to my fleet. Renting a hangar in Great Falls, Montana, I installed a five-hundred gallon chemical tank with three six-inch dump valves in each airplane. A test flight had to be made to determine the minimum engine- out controllable speed and the time needed to dump the load, thereby reducing the gross weight to allow single-engine climb. For the flight test, we filled the chemical tanks with five-hundred gallons of water. This brought our gross takeoff weight to around 11,000 pounds. Normal gross weight was 7,800 pounds.

After a normal takeoff, I climbed to three-thousand feet above ground level (AGL) and started a test to determine minimum engine-out controllable speed. With the left engine at zero thrust and the right engine at climb power, I started reducing the airspeed. With almost full-right rudder and near-stall speed, I estimated the engine-out controllable airspeed. A stall at this gross weight and only three thousand feet AGL would probably be fatal. Next, I dumped the water load and determined that it would take about six seconds to reduce the gross weight, for a safe single-engine climb.

The test concluded that the pilot had to obtain at least a 106 miles-per-hour climb airspeed after takeoff, in order dump the load and continue a climb, with an engine-out and prop feathered. Between takeoff speed and 106 miles-per-hour, an engine-out would result in a crash. I knew that such a high gross load would put high structural stress on the aircraft, but it would be a few years before I became concerned. There were reports of center section problems, and I decided it was time to calculate the load factor at this high gross weight. At the normal gross weight, the aircraft had a safe wing-load factor of 9G's (9 times the normal gross weight). At a gross weight of 11,000 pounds, the maximum safe wing-load factor is reduced to 2G's. When I stopped to think that an aircraft in a level 60-degree bank has a 2G wing load, it scared the hell out of me. That's when I decided to sell the two twin Beechcrafts.

They had served us well for a few trouble-free years. We had a very large U. S. Forest Service spray contract at Mount Pocono, Pennsylvania, and another job in northeast Minnesota. The Bureau of Land Management provided some large grasshopper spray jobs in Wyoming and Montana. A full page ad in the "Montana Farmer's Stockmen's Newspaper" produced several large ranch jobs at 10,000 to 30,000 acres each.

An F7F and twin engine Beechcraft in Great Falls, MT

It was time to expand into forest fire business, so I bought a surplus Navy F7F. It was located about 50 miles west of Phoenix, Arizona. When I arrived at the airport to fly it back to Great Falls, Montana, with a fuel stop in Salt Lake City, Utah, the mechanic had it all ready to go. The F7F had two Pratt & Whitney R2800 engines, rated at 2000 horsepower each and, a fuselage almost wide enough for one pilot. There was no flight manual to provide flight information. I was sitting in the cockpit, with a mechanic standing on the wing,

173

showing me where everything was, when a navy pilot came walking by. I yelled, "Have you ever flown this plane?" He hollered back, "Yes, but it was a long time ago." I said, "I have to fly it out of here, and I can't find any information on it." He said, "If you lose an engine on takeoff, come back on the good engine quickly, and don't do a split S because it will hit the sound barrier."

With that information, I started both engines and taxied out for takeoff. Applying 56 inches of takeoff power, the airplane jumped into the air. After takeoff to the south, I had to make a 180-degree turn to head to Salt Lake City, so I rolled into a 30-degree bank and started checking the engine instruments. Suddenly, I saw an instrument rotating fast. It was the altimeter, and I was passing through 16,500 feet, and had not yet completed my 180-degree turn. I cut the power and quickly descended to below 10,000 feet. I would learn later that this was the fastest climbing prop plane ever built.

Normal fuel consumption for the F7F was 180 gallons an hour, so to save money, I was slow-flying, which was still very fast. After refueling in Salt Lake City, I took off for Great Falls, Montana, and soon noticed that the right engine was leaving a trail of white smoke, and the oil pressure had begun to drop. My plan, upon reaching Great Falls, was to make a high-speed fly-by, followed by a vertical climb. Not wanting to make a single-engine landing in a strange airplane, I made a quick landing, disappointing the people waiting to see the show.

A short time later, a Wyoming operator friend was killed in one of his B-17's, while fighting a fire in Wyoming. His accident changed my mind, and I decided not to get into the fire-fighting business. After sitting for a year or two, the F7F was sold to Cal Butler in Redmond, OR. He used it for several years fighting fires. He later sold it, and it ended up in a museum in England.

There was one grasshopper spray job I'll never forget. After spraying seventeen square miles on a ranch located just west of Manhattan, Montana, the owner failed to pay his bill. He said, "You have some misses, so bring your airplane back over and spray the misses." I flew the Pacer back to Manhattan, and he had his foreman get into the airplane and show me where the misses were. The foreman pointed out the starting line and an area that I was not contracted to spray. Prior to starting the job, I had advised the owner to spray that area. This man not only owned a huge ranch, but also a large cattle feed lot and the Manhattan bank. It became clear to me that I was going have to sue to get my money, so I hired a Bozeman, Montana, lawyer who had retired from the FBI.

The trial brought wide attention because it was the first trial involving agriculture aviation. Just before the trial started, he offered to settle for a sum less than what was owed, but I refused his offer. There was testimony that he had asked the government to spray a few years earlier, and unknown to anyone, a Montana State College Biology teacher had been counting the grasshoppers per square yard for several years on his ranch. He not only testified as to the yearly count, but he also gave the biological names of all the grasshoppers he found. Then the judge asked, "What did you find after it was sprayed?" He said he found one grasshopper and gave its biological name. The judge said, "That biological name was not on your previous list. Where did that grasshopper come from?" He answered, "Judge, I don't know where that grasshopper came from."

We won, and the lawyer and I left the courthouse and walked down Bozeman's main street and back to the courthouse. We couldn't take more than a few steps without someone shaking his hand and congratulating him. When we got back to the courthouse, he said, "Let's do it again." Apparently, taking this man to court had been long-neglected, because it seemed as everyone was glad to see him lose.

During one conversation with this rancher, he said that he was going to Helena for a farewell meeting for outgoing Montana Governor, Hugo Aronson, and that Barry Goldwater would be there. I did not tell him that I knew Goldwater. That night in Helena, I walked up behind Goldwater, while he and the Governor were sitting at the speaker's podium, and tapped on his shoulder. He turned around and said, "Tom Herrod, what are you doing in Helena, Montana? You are supposed to be in Little Rock, Arkansas." It had been twelve years since we had been together drinking his Old Crow. Looking down on the first row was the old rancher with his mouth open in surprise.

CHAPTER 30
Chemical Business 1958 - 1960

The U.S. Forest Service was letting large spray contracts using DDT to kill spruce bud worms. They needed a contractor to formulate the DDT and load the airplanes. Since I had portable storage tanks that held 20,000 gallons, 200 gallons-per-minute pumps, meters and hoses, and a desire to make maximum use of my assets, it was time to bid on contracts to formulate DDT.

Portable chemical tank

One-hundred percent DDT is a white power insecticide that came in 100-pound sacks. The powder was turned into a liquid by mixing it with cycle oil that was heated to over 100 degrees Fahrenheit. Diesel fuel was added to provide the desired amount of DDT per gallon.

My first contract was for the U.S. Forest Service at the Bozeman, Montana, airport, and it was one that I will never forget. The cycle oil and diesel fuel came from a refinery in Billings, Montana. We had trouble keeping the DDT in solution. Starting early one Monday morning, I worked around the clock until Friday afternoon. By that time, I was stumbling around, but none of the help was paying any attention to me. Finally, they took me to a motel where I slept for 48 hours. Later, I learned that we were using the wrong cycle oil, and that the cycle oil we should have used was from a refinery in Texas City, Texas.

A short time later, the U.S. Forest Service let contracts to spray over a hundred- and-fifty-thousand acres of forest land in northern Minnesota, Wisconsin, and Michigan. With my learning experience in making DDT in Bozeman, Montana, I was ready and trained for this big contract. In Superior, Wisconsin, I leased the Carnegie dock because it had three railroad tracks. There was a railroad tank car manufacturer in Superior that supplied an insulated tank car that could be heated with steam. It was placed on the first track. A boxcar load of one-hundred-pound sacks of DDT was placed on the second track. A conveyor belt was placed between the insulated tank car and the box car. A couple of tank cars of cycle oil were shipped out of Texas City, Texas, and were placed on the third track. A seven-thousand-gallon tanker truck and driver were leased out of Bemidji, Minnesota. A group of unemployed longshoremen was contracted to load the one-hundred-pound sacks of DDT into the heated cycle oil tank car, and manage the two- hundred-gallon-a-minute pumps, meters and four-inch hoses. With this setup, we were ready to start formulating DDT.

Everything was going fine until the tanker pulled into the oil refinery to get a load of diesel oil. It was a short distance from the Carnegie dock. His arrival broke up a big argument between the Superior, WI, teamsters and the Duluth, MN, teamsters. They came over to our tanker and asked, "Who owns this tanker?" Our driver said, "It's none of your damned business." Understand that this driver was a huge man who looked like an enormous gorilla. When the loaded tanker returned to our dock, the teamsters followed, but they stopped at the gate. The driver told me the story, and I went down to the gate and said, "Gentlemen, what is your problem?" One answered, "We think that tanker is illegal, and we have called the state police." I said, "Gentlemen, I am from Montana, and I don't know anything about your problems in Wisconsin, but, when the police get here, tell them to come on through the gate, and if one of you comes through this gate, I will shoot to kill!"

All hell broke loose! The Superior Mayor got involved, and I told him, "I am from Montana and I don't know anything about your problems in Wisconsin. I have over a hundred-thousand dollars on this dock, and I don't intend to have it destroyed." Not only the Mayor, but also the railroad company that owned the dock and the tank car company, then became involved. The problem disappeared as quickly as it had appeared, and nobody ever knew that this Montanan was not armed.

While I was at the Carnegie dock formulating DDT, a forest service person said that the state of Minnesota wanted to know if I would sell them seven-thousand gallons of DDT. I agreed to the sale, and the state of Minnesota called and said they would have a tanker there in the morning to pick up the DDT. The next morning, instead of a tanker, a two-and-one-half ton truck arrived with a one-thousand-gallon tank to pick up DDT. The smallest pump and meter we had was two-hundred-gallons per minute, and the smallest hose was four inches. We would have to disassemble everything just to load the thousand-gallon tank. I explained the problem to the Minnesota contract officer, and he agreed to pay an extra eighty dollars a load. There was a small pump on their truck, so by buying a few feet of one-and-a-half inch hose, and using their pump, we no longer had to disassemble our plant to load their tank six more times.

After the last load of DDT was picked up, the Minnesota contract officer came to pay his bill. I recognized him as the one who had rejected my successful bid on a large spray contract a couple of years prior, but he did not remember me. I handed him my bill. He was expecting a bill based on the price the U. S. Forest Service was paying. I said, "You don't think you are going to pay the same price for seven-thousand gallons as the Forest Service pays for over one-hundred-and-fifty-thousand gallons. The price you are paying is far below what you could get anywhere else." He said, "Since you used our pump to load the DDT, are you going to charge for loading?" Without saying a word, I handed him his written agreement to pay eighty dollars a load. As he handed me the check, I said, "You don't remember me do you? I am the guy from Montana who was the successful bidder of the spray contact, and you canceled the contract after I had spent three-thousand dollars to prepare the bid." To say the least, he left and was not a happy camper.

At that time, the contract business was getting larger and larger, and very profitable. The farm-spraying business was becoming less and less enjoyable. Part of my life philosophy is that a person must enjoy what he is doing, or it's not worth doing. I was tired of people complaining about the aircraft noise and tree damage, so I closed the farm spray business, sold the single-engine spray planes and moved everything to my favorite city, Billings, Montana.

CHAPTER 31
The Last Contracts 1961

The next addition to our fleet was a surplus Navy PV-2. I built a 1,400 gallon chemical tank in the bomb bay, and with two 2,000 horse-power engines and a 600-foot swath, it became a very effective spray plane. The first bid was for a very large contract to spray sagebrush in Oregon. After being named the successful bidder, I received a phone call from Washington, D.C. They told me that a person would be arriving the next day at 1500 to inspect my airplanes. When he got off the airplane, instead of inspecting the airplanes, he wanted to go to his hotel. The next day, he did his inspection and turned me down. I called a couple of competitors and found out that this guy was an alcoholic who had been causing a lot of trouble. Having already spent a lot of money preparing the bid, I phoned the U.S. Senator from Montana, Mike Mansfield, and told him the story. The next day, another man arrived and said, "I'm not sure what this all about, but this morning I was called into the Secretary of Interior's office. Senator Mike Mansfield was there, and they told me to go to Billings, Montana, and clear up this mess." He inspected all the airplanes, and I was awarded the contract.

Lockheed PV-2

Things really started to move. Our truck and trailer with two large tanks, pumps, meters, and hoses left Billings for Oregon. A tanker truck loaded with 100-octane aviation fuel left Salt Lake City, UT and tankers with 245T chemical and diesel oil left Portland, OR. Our two twin-engine Beechcraft headed for Burns, OR, and the new PV-2 spray plane headed for Lakeview, OR.

About fifteen miles south of Burns, OR, we made an airstrip for the two twin-engine Beechcraft. The job got off to a bad start. The first morning, it was raining, and I told everyone that we would not be spraying that day, and I drove into town. I sat down in a restaurant to have breakfast. Just after ordering, a strange feeling came over me that something was very wrong back at the airstrip. It was the same feeling I had had a few years earlier, before the sheriff called to tell me about that fatal spray plane crash. I jumped up, put some money on the table, ran out, got into my pick up, and drove at top speed back to the airstrip. As I drove within the sight of the airstrip, I saw one of the airplanes standing on its nose. One of the pilots had tried to takeoff on that muddy airstrip. They had tied a rope to the tail wheel and were about to pull the tail down. I stopped them, because this could have caused damage to the fuselage. After gently lowering the tail, we ordered two new props, installed them, and the airplane was back in service in forty-eight hours. With the two twin-engine Beechcraft sprayers spraying five- hundred acres per flight, it did not take too long to finish the Burn's job, and then it was off to Lakeview, OR.

The large acreage to be sprayed was about thirty miles east of Lakeview, about three miles south of Adel, and up to the Nevada state line. There was a dry lake bed next to it, which made a good airfield, and it lowered my bid price. The problem was that recent rains had left six inches of water over it, so we had to make a new airstrip. The ground was almost like powder. To make the strip useable each morning, we had to spray water on it all night long. Our water truck, with a thousand-gallon tank, hauled water from sunset to daylight the next morning, spraying the strip.

This was close to a half-million-dollar contract. The profit on it was so low that it caused the IRS to come in and audit our books. When they finished, they owed me over four-hundred dollars. This was one of several IRS audits, and after each audit, they owed me money. I told my accountant, "When I get an IRS audit, I should owe them money. It looks like you are working for them, not me."

The next contract was some acreage south of Buffalo, WY. Only the PV-2 was needed for this job. As usual, everything was set in motion. My insurance agent called and said, "The state of Wyoming has a law that requires only state workmen's compensation be used, and they will not insure you!" Then I called the head of the Wyoming State Insurance Department, and he said, "Mr. Herrod, you bring your planes on in, do the job, and then get out." Since it was a small job and I would be doing all the flying, it was all go.

On my first load, about thirty miles south of Buffalo, I was having trouble with the spray valve fully opening, but rather than take the time to fix it, I put my teenage son in the back of the airplane to make sure that the valve fully opened. On the first pass, we were spraying uphill in the bottom of a canyon, when a loud bang from the right engine shook the airplane. I immediately added power to the left engine, and started climbing up and out of that canyon. As we passed over the east ridge, I feathered the prop on the right engine. The airplane was filling with smoke. The chase plane was yelling, "You are on fire, you are on fire!" I dropped down to ground level with intensions of bellying in, jumping out, and running like hell. I finally decided that there was no fire and started trying to climb enough to clear the saddle that I-25 passes through just south of Buffalo. I still had a full load of chemical, and since it was worth a few thousand dollars, I didn't want to dump it. As we reached the saddle, with almost full left rudder and getting very close to engine-out controllable speed, I yelled, "DUMP!" My mechanic, sitting in the right seat with his hand already on the dump valve, dumped the load. Immediately, over ten-thousand pounds of chemical was dumped. The single engine landing at the Buffalo Airport was no problem.

We were thankful to have survived because, when a pilot goes up a canyon and loses an engine, he is not likely to be able to make a one-hundred-and-eighty-degree turn and get out. If he is flying down a canyon, there is no problem. We thought we had no problem because one of the twin-engine Beechcraft sprayers could finish the job, but about an hour after we landed, several government cars drove up to the airplane. We had been awarded a contract to spray thousands of acres.

We knew that we had to get that PV-2 back in the air fast. I called Phoenix, Arizona, and bought a surplus engine from the firewall forward. I had them put it into a U-Haul truck with two drivers, and instructed them not to stop until they reached Buffalo, WY. The contractor who was building I-25 sent his crane over to lift the damaged engine off the plane and lift the new engine on. The plane was ready to fly in a little over forty-eight hours.

Part of the new contract acreage was seventeen miles long. The longest run I had ever had before was two or three miles long. Just think about it: laying a six-hundred foot-swath, flying at one-hundred-and-eighty miles-per-hour for seventeen miles. That is making money fast! The downside was that I had to spend three or four hours a day flying the chase plane over this land in order to know the terrain well enough to not overlap the swaths.

When this contract was finished, it was time to quit the contract spraying business. Working in a business that is so dangerous that there is no way to cover the liabilities with insurance, makes the risks far exceed the rewards, no matter how much profit is made. The aircraft were sold, and it was time to develop a new business.

CHAPTER 32
Airline Pilot School 1961-1969

I rented some unused space in the basement of the Billings Airport Terminal and bought a very sophisticated link trainer (a WWII flight simulator). Frontier Airlines had fifty-three pilots domiciled in Billings. They were flying DC-3's, and I contracted with Frontier Airlines to provide pilot recurrent training for those pilots using the link trainer. They were a great bunch of pilots, and they taught me as much as I taught them.

All my spare time was used to write a home study "Private Pilots Course" that sold for twenty-five dollars. Every Friday night I would give a two-hour lecture in a meeting room in the basement of the Billings Airport terminal, and I charged five dollars per student. We always had a full house. It took me forty hours to prepare for each lecture, but it was worth it. This led to a three-day accelerated ground school for passing the FAA written exams for private, commercial or instrument licenses. This led to a six- month airline pilot school that lasted eight years, with a new class starting every three months, and we placed over a hundred pilots on major airlines.

Training Aircraft

Piper Comanche 180 (PA-24)   **Piper Cherokee 140 (PA-28)**

The airline pilot school courses were designed to teach in the fastest way possible, and in a way that the student would not only have complete understanding of the subject, but also have the ability to use the knowledge. I used a whole-part-whole approach on a block of subject matter. This gave the student the big picture of the material he was about to learn. Next, small blocks were presented, each followed by a question. The question was not for examination purposes, but was used to hold the student's attention. The students knew that a question was coming, and they didn't want to miss it. With this method of teaching, we proved that we could hold a student's attention for twelve hours in a day.

Writing an airline pilot course is one thing, but starting an airline pilot school is another thing. It involved putting at risk thousands of dollars, and while some of my past businesses had made large amounts of money, two had caused me to go broke. For the airline pilot school, I decided to limit my risk to one-thousand dollars. The plan was to go into colleges and universities to find students who had personal profiles that we wanted as airline pilot students. They would have to go to school twelve hours a day, five days a weeks, for six months. At the end of the first three months, they would be interviewed and tested by the airlines. If accepted by an airline, they would spend the next three months finishing the course with a commercial pilot's license with instrument rating, multiengine rating, flight instructors rating, and ground instructor rating. They also would have passed the airline transport rating written exam.

Starting with Northwest Airlines, I flew to Minneapolis, MN, and laid out my plan to Ben Griggs, Vice President of flight operations. He not only bought the plan, but he also said, "We'll send a person from personnel to help you." Then he said, "Let's go and tell Nyrop what we plan to do." Donald Nyrop was President of Northwest Airlines. He remembered me from back in the 50's, when he was head of the National Civil Aviation Board and I was helping to write the FAR's for agriculture aircraft.

Then, I flew to Chicago, to meet with the Vice-President of United Airlines. He invited me to their 0900 executive meeting. It lasted over an hour, and I was very impressed at how detailed all reports were presented. He was very pleased with my approach to pilot training, and said that he would send a chief pilot and someone from personnel to test and interview at the end of the first three months of training.

The next step was to finish the school catalog, get it out to all the colleges and universities, and then write a contract agreement. The course would cost five-thousand dollars. Two-thousand dollars had to be in a bank escrow account two weeks before class started. Ten days before class started, five-hundred dollars would be paid to the school and was not refundable. During the first three weeks of classes, the school or the student could break the contract, and the students would receive the balance of the two-thousand dollars. Otherwise, the money was given to the school and was nonrefundable. Not once did we ever have a student break the contract or leave before finishing the course.

The next step was to go the colleges and universities to interview and test prospective students. It started with them filling out an application that allowed us to screen the student. We required at least two years of college, and each student had to meet our age, height and weight requirements. If he met our requirements, he got an interview. Once past the interview, he was given four hours of written tests. Once the tests were evaluated, we had a complete profile on the student. We knew his reading speed and comprehension, his math level and mechanical aptitude. We even had a personality inventory by using the MMPI test, which was interpreted by a PhD psychologist. The final test was an FAA first class physical exam as prescribed by Mayo Clinic. Their eye sight had to be 20-20 uncorrected. No prior arrest record was accepted, and one very good student applicant was turned down because of multiple speeding tickets.

Two weeks before the first class started, I flew to Vero Beach, Florida, to bring back a new Piper Cherokee PA-28 from the Piper factory. To stay within my one- thousand dollar budget, I borrowed seventy-five-percent of the plane's retail cost, and also got a twenty-five-percent dealer discount. Two weeks after the starting date of the first class, escrow money was moved into my account, and I was already over twenty- thousand dollars ahead. After all these years, I had finally learned how to start a business.

During the first three days, the students were given twelve hours of lecture a day. Class started each morning at 0800 and ended at 2200 that night. At the end of the first three days, students had been exposed to aerodynamics, aviation weather, navigation, federal aviation regulations, and air traffic procedures. The aviation weather office, control tower, and flight service station were in the same terminal as our school, so they had a chance to get acquainted and see everything in action. They had been exposed to everything they were going to learn in the next six months.

Each day from then on, they had four hours of lecture, four hours with a flying lesson in the airplane, plus a flight simulator lesson, and four hours of supervised study. During their study period, there was an instructor present to quickly answer any question, as we did not want them using their time researching something that the instructor could explain quickly. They were encouraged to use our self-taught speed-reading course to improve their reading speed and comprehension. Airline pilots receive a lot of material to read.

From the beginning, I had to buy another Piper Cherokee PA-28, hire two flight instructors, and an accountant to keep records. There was so much material to be printed that I bought a used AB Dick offset printing machine. The link trainer was replaced with a computerized flight simulator. It was a five-thousand-pound analog computer simulator, complete with sound and feel of a real airplane. It had an instructor station with a map plotting system.

I'll never forget walking by the simulator one day, just as a new student was getting out, looking very pale. I thought he was sick, about ready to vomit. I said, "What's the matter?" He said, "I just missed that VOR approach." This was a new student, without any prior flying time, who had not even made his first solo flight, and he did not know that VOR approaches are normally very advanced training. It made me realize how advanced our training system was.

Normally, we would expect to solo a student after around eight hours of dual instruction, but when one is training at a controlled airport, and in traffic with very heavy aircraft, it usually takes a little more dual instruction. Large, heavy aircraft leave violent, and very dangerous, wake turbulence that can destroy small aircraft. Our students had to be taught how to avoid the wake turbulence; all the air traffic control procedures; and how to use the radio for ground control, tower control, departure control and approach control.

At the end of the first three months, Northwest Airlines flew each student to Minneapolis, MN, for testing and interviews. A United Airlines chief pilot from Seattle, WA, and a gentleman from the personnel department arrived in Billings for testing and interviews. Three were selected by United Airlines, and the rest were selected by

Northwest Airlines. All they had to do was get through another three months of intensive twelve-hour-a-day training.

Our two aircraft were flying around the clock. There was one three-month period when the aircraft averaged 20.3 hours per day. When the weather turned IFR (Instrument Flight Rules), we kept flying and welcomed the opportunity to train in real instrument weather. The FAA issued us a special waiver for the one-hundred-hour aircraft inspection. If the hundred-hour inspection came due after 1200, we could fly the plane until 0800 the next morning. At that time, two mechanics and three students would complete the hundred hour inspection in a few hours. When an engine overhaul came due, we had a new replacement, overhauled engine ready, and the aircraft was back flying in a very short time.

With two classes in full operation, we added another airplane to the fleet: a nearly new, four-place Piper Comanche PA 24. With a six-hundred-mile range, it made an excellent cross-country trainer. The instrument panel and radios were replaced to make it fully IFR qualified. Four advanced students could take very long trips and experience flying into major airports around the country. We did not have to worry about the students forgetting to lower the landing gear. Although all the Cherokee airplanes had a fixed gear, we had equipped them with a landing gear lever, complete with gear-up horn. Students had always used a gear-down lever in their landing check list.

There was just one FAA flight inspector in Billings. To lower his work load, they made me a flight examiner. When the first class of students came up for their commercial flight check ride, a very disturbing fact became very clear: When I asked the student to do a seven-hundred-twenty-degree steep turn, he would properly clear us from other traffic, then look at the instrument panel, and do a perfect turn. He did the same for chandelles and lazy eights. A disturbing fact struck me: I had trained all these students, and none could or would fly visually. I flew to Minneapolis, met with Ben Griggs, Vice President of Northwest flight operations, and explained my deep concern. He said, "Don't worry. That is the way we want them trained."

I made a trip to Denver to check with the head of training for United Airlines, to find out how our three new airline pilots had done in United's new-hire training. United had put their new-pilot hires through their new-hire class and had given them time in their DC-6 simulator. They were the only airline that gave these pilots left-seat touch-and go-time in a DC-6. We wanted to determine how qualified our students were, compared to high-time, experienced pilots. We picked three Air Force pilots with a lot of time in heavy aircraft, and compared their grades with our three pilots'. The top two were my pilots; the third was an Air Force pilot; fourth was my pilot; and the last two were Air Force. The results surprised them and made me very happy. I asked one of my trained pilots, "How can you, having flown nothing but small airplanes, get into a large, heavy DC-6 and have no trouble flying it?" He said, "You taught us that a given power and a given attitude will produce given results. Once we had the numbers for the DC-6, there was no problem."

One morning a student came back from the flight line to report that the plane he was to fly, that had an instructor and student aboard, was fifteen minutes overdue. Immediately, that strange feeling came over me: Something bad had happened. Rushing upstairs, I had flight service and the tower try to raise them on the radio. There was no response. Another instructor and I got in an airplane and went searching for them. We flew northwest, and about fifteen miles from the airport, we found our plane crashed in a way that there could have been no survivors. That day we lost a student and a flight instructor. As regrettable as this loss was, we were thankful that it was the only accident we had, considering that the airplanes flew over twenty-thousand hours, much of it single-engine night and actual instrument.

It was always my objective to teach in a way that the student would learn in the fastest possible way, and be taught to use what he had learned. The airlines were using a student response system which was an improvement over the system I was using. The system included a back screen projector system, a podium, and hand-response units. The podium not only controlled the entire system, but it also had a complete list of student names, and lights by their names, to show the instructor their answers to questions that appeared on the back screen. The back screen had a projector with slides and a set of mirrors. The student hand-unit had push buttons and lights for "make selection", "A", "B", or "C", "right" or "wrong".

Our system of teaching was basically the same, except we used reams and reams of paper. A conversion to an electronic response system was going to take a lot of time, and I had no spare time left. So, for the summer, I rented office space, equipped it with desks and typewriters, and hired four schoolteachers for the summer, to convert instructional material to the new system. Three of the teachers had aviation experience, and one (without aviation experience) was to write a course on "How to Teach", as all the students were to have instructor ratings. By the end of the first three weeks, the three with aviation experience had given up and left. The other, with no aviation experience, had finished the "How to Teach" course. She had written the course that conformed to my teaching system. She spent the balance of the summer listening to the lectures, and making projector slides to convert our teaching to the new system. Her name was Judy Rudin, and she was teaching in Great Falls, Montana.

One day Judy said, "I've never flown, and I would like to take a lesson." I said, "OK, when the weather gets so bad that we cannot fly the students, you can have an airplane and an instructor." That summer the accountant left and Judy took over his work and all of the bookkeeping records and accounting. When the school year started, she headed back to Great Falls to teach, but every Friday night, she took the airline to Billings, and would fly back Sunday night to teach in Great Falls. Each weekend she would take care of all the records and accounting. She would also try to get some flying time. The next summer she moved to Billings, and worked in the Airline Pilot School as a ground instructor. If the weather got too bad for students, she got an airplane and an instructor. She took a public school teaching position in the Billings Public School System and worked part-time in our pilot school. By the end of the public school year, she had earned a commercial pilot's license with instrument rating, plus flight and ground instructor licenses, and she had become one of my full-time flight and ground instructors.

A year or two after my first wife had died with bone cancer, I married Judy. Some said that I married her to lower my overhead. Together, we made a great team and could take over a lecture even in the middle of a sentence.

There had been only two times during my lifetime that the nation had faced a pilot shortage. The first was during World War II, and the second was during the Vietnam War, starting in the early '60's. By the end of the '60's, with war ending and hundreds of pilots being released from the military, it was time to be realistic about the supply-demand effect on my product. Add to this the fact that I had loaned many students the money for the last three months of training, which would provide income for the next three to five years. Thank goodness that in the beginning, I had the foresight to change my accounting system from accrual to a cash accounting system. In addition to these factors, the airport manager had said they were going to raise my rent. I said "If you raise my rent, I'll close the school." He did, and I did.

Every three months, when United Airlines would come to Billings, they would ask me to move the school to one of their hubs, so, we moved everything to Denver, Colorado. Not being ready to start a new flight school, we put the flight simulator in storage and set up a classroom in a motel near Stapleton Field. Each weekend we would hold a three-day, accelerated ground school. It proved very successful. People could fly in from all over and attend our school on Friday, Saturday and Sunday, with a guarantee to pass the FAA written exam. We never had to make a refund. One morning the phone rang; it was my accountant in Great Falls, Montana. He said, "I've got your taxes ready, and you had better sit down." I said, "I think I can take it standing up." He told me how much I owed the state of Montana, how much I owed the state of Colorado, and how much I owed the I R S. Judy and I were completely dumfounded and just sat silent for forty-five minutes. Then I said, "OK, I've had it! By the time the IRS gets through with us, the reward is not worth the risk. I am going to find a way to make our entire cost of living a tax deduction, and we are only going to make enough money to cover our cost of living."

We sold the two Cherokees; one had over nine-thousand, six-hundred hours, and the other had over sixty-seven-hundred hours. The Comanche was still parked in Billings, Montana. It had been depreciated down so low that I didn't want to pay taxes on the gain.

We established a residence in Billings, Montana, for tax purposes, and bought a wrecked Airstream travel trailer. We took it to our empty airport hangar and quickly rebuilt it. Then we were off, following the sun, and we could hold a week-end ground school, wherever we wanted to go. For the next three years, we traveled all over the country and held twelve ground schools a year; we still had to pay taxes each year.

Bert Dowd, western sales manager for Airstream, was impressed with our skill and speed in rebuilding the wrecked Airstream, and he wanted us to take an Airstream dealership. We were not interested, but over a three-year period, he would often contact us with an offer to take a dealership in some major city. One summer, as we were relaxing for two weeks at Big Fork, Montana, on the shore of beautiful Flathead Lake, we saw a new Airstream parked next to us. It was Bert, and he said, "We are cancelling the Billings dealer and want you to take the dealership." The very same day, my son called from Billings and said, "There is a man here who wants to trade some commercial property on the interstate for your Comanche."

I borrowed a plane from a friend, and we flew to Billings to inspect the property. It was a perfect location for an RV dealership. There was a house that made a perfect office, and a shop that was large enough to hold two Airstreams. We made the trade, and for the first time in many years I did not own a single airplane. During the previous three years, without keeping my pilot proficiency up, I was not the pilot I had been. For a professional pilot, this can be fatal. Add to this, my age was a little short of sixty; it was time to leave the profession I had loved since the age of thirteen.

CHAPTER 33
Looking Back

How does one explain thirty years of flying, with over eighteen-thousand hours flying time, accident free, and not ever scratching an airplane? Consider that during WW II, I spent almost a year flying the CBI Hump, over the world's highest mountains with the world's worst weather, and with some of the route behind enemy lines. Then, add thirteen years crop spraying, where pilot fatalities were two percent per year. There had to be some luck involved. In my opinion, it is foolish to depend on luck as a factor leading to a successful, prosperous and happy life.

What are the important factors that lead to a successful, prosperous and happy life? I believe that the answer can be broken down into two categories: education and the basic philosophy that a person lives by.

Education:

My education in aviation started with building and flying model airplanes, and spending one summer becoming an aircraft and engine mechanic. While in college, I worked nights at the airport as a mechanic. The study of physics provided not only the understanding of the stress and strain of forces on the aircraft, but also how to calculate them. Then, there was the training I received from a very experienced Consolidated Aircraft Test Pilot. Using what he taught me, when writing an instructor's manual for B-25's training, helped save lives. Whatever path one takes in life, he can never stop learning.

Basic Philosophy:

Having the right basic philosophy is essential for success. One summer, at the age of thirteen, I got to spend a week at Hendrix College in Conway, AR, with college professors as mentors; I started developing my basic philosophy. Let me explain some of my philosophical rules and how they led me to a successful, prosperous, happy life.

Honesty: The people one does business with know when they are dealing with an honest person. I could move thousands and thousands of dollars of material with just a phone call.

Responsibility: This is a necessary assumption that must be taken to successfully complete any task that is undertaken. One must be willing, able and capable of assuming responsibility. People we do business with expect us to be responsible.

Dependability: To be successful, people must know that they can depend on us.

Plan Ahead: A person must always think at least five years ahead because, if he doesn't know where he is going, he can't get there. He can change his plan, but the new plan must extend out five years. Looking ahead five years at the entire world is also necessary in order to make good and timely decisions.

Innovation: It pays to find a faster, lower cost, or better way of accomplishing, a task. Look at every task through the eyes of an innovator.

Risk / Reward: All decisions made in life involve weighing the risk against reward. Although this is done subconsciously in our daily decisions with little thought, any important decision requires a thorough study of the resulting risk and reward. It is wise to always limit the risk.

Entrepreneurship: As a non-governmental employee, one must always make an employer a profit. If he doesn't, they don't need him. So, why shouldn't he work for himself? There is only one reason I would work for someone else: He knows something I need to know and he is willing to teach me.

Love of work: In order to achieve maximum success, a person must enjoy his work. It is what he wants to talk about, what he wants to read about, and something he looks forward to doing each day.

Communication: Effective communication skills are the most important factors to be learned and used to maximize success. My study started in 1937, when I bought Dale Carnegie's book, "How to Win Friends and Influence People". By using its teachings, this teenage paperboy kept winning sales contests, and during my business years, I was able to work directly with executives of the large airlines.

Carnegie's book is a must-read for anyone wanting to get ahead in this world.

I finish my story by sharing my basic philosophical tenets. They not only led me through a successful, prosperous and happy life, but also my work made hundreds of farmers and ranchers more money by increasing their yields. Lastly, over a hundred of my students entered into very lucrative airline pilot careers.

CPSIA information can be obtained at www.ICGtesting.com
Printed in the USA
LVOW13s1733131013

356719LV00027B/1196/P